Measure for Measure

Measure for Measure

Using Portfolios in K–8 Mathematics

Therese M. Kuhs

HEINEMANN
Portsmouth, NH

Heinemann
A division of Reed Elsevier Inc.
361 Hanover Street
Portsmouth, NH 03801-3912

Offices and agents throughout the world

Library of Congress Cataloging-in-Publication Data

Kuhs, Therese.
    Measure for measure : using portfolios in K–8 mathematics / Therese M. Kuhs.
        p.   cm.
    Includes bibliographical references.
    ISBN 0-435-07135-1 (acid-free paper)
    1. Mathematics—Study and teaching.   2. Portfolios in education.   I. Title.
    QA20.P67K84   1997
    510'.71—dc21   96-49303
                                                                              CIP

Editors: Leigh Peake and Victoria Merecki
Production: Melissa L. Inglis
Cover design: Michael Leary
Manufacturing: Louise Richardson

Printed in the United States of America on acid-free paper
00 99 98 97   DA   1 2 3 4 5 6 7 8 9

Contents

Contents

To the Reader

During the past four years, I have been doing research for this book. I was trying to find *the* two or three classrooms that I would use to tell the story of success with portfolio assessment in mathematics. Conversations with many elementary and middle school teachers helped me realize that the story has as many plots as there are teachers using portfolios.

I owe a great debt to many teachers. Some allowed me to be a frequent visitor in their classrooms and didn't mind when I asked their students questions. Others were willing to try out things I thought would work—and sometimes they did work! Others talked to me, told me their stories, or inspired me with their writings or presentations at meetings. All of these teachers have given me a story to tell that I hope will be helpful to others who want to use portfolios in the mathematics classroom. The names of students, teachers, and others in this book are all fictitious. Any resemblance to persons you know is accidental.

The stories in this book are attempts to portray the reality that teachers face when trying to use portfolios. I used anecdotes and examples in this book for two purposes. Some of them are stories that help carry important messages about portfolio use. Others are model conversations and interactions. The conversations between teachers and students are to demonstrate strategies for involving children in the assessment process in a meaningful way. The conversations with families are designed to suggest ways of communicating information about new assessment approaches to those who are not education professionals.

In all the years I have worked on portfolio assessment, I have found that teachers always ask for "samples," but when samples are produced they quickly see that no sample will adapt itself completely to their classroom. In fact, I deliberately avoid giving complete samples because I do not believe that portfolio systems can be transplanted from one classroom to another. As individual teachers develop and implement their own plans for portfolio use, what evolves is each teacher's personal statement about what is important for students to learn. At the same time, the teacher makes a commitment to monitor student progress in these important matters.

What this book offers is a variety of planning models that suggest different ways teachers might use portfolios. These models also demonstrate how portfolio requirements can be communicated to students. The discussion outlines how teachers can establish evaluation plans that makes sense in their own classrooms.

The approach I have taken is to provide descriptions of individual success stories that together show what a multifaceted and powerful tool a portfolio is, and what the use of portfolios in mathematics might look like. Although my discussions and examples illustrate mathematics portfolios for elementary and middle school grades, the strategies and guidelines proposed may be useful to teachers of other subjects and at higher grade lelvels. I hope that what I have to share will help teachers bring the best of portfolio experiences to the learners in their classrooms.

Therese M. Kuhs

Chapter 1

What Is a Portfolio?
Ten Pounds of Potatoes in a
Five-Pound Bag!

By the third week of school, I was ready to give portfolios a try in my first-grade classroom. I had a portfolio workshop leader's advice that students should be responsible for managing the collections to keep the teacher from being overwhelmed with paperwork. The leader also claimed that student involvement provides an important opportunity for learning. I asked myself if any of that made sense in a first-grade classroom. Two months later I had a story to share.

I knew the first thing I needed to do was to teach the children how to manage their portfolios and keep the collection. I decided I would also use the experience as an occasion to teach a mathematics lesson about the order of numbers and a social studies lesson about how to find particular places in the community. I used regular file folders and numbered one group of folders from 1 to 12 with a blue marker and the other group from 1 to 12 in orange. I told the children the colors would be street names and kept the blue and orange folders in different boxes, a blue box and an orange one. I told the children that the numbers would be their "house numbers" on either Blue Street or Orange Street. It was their job to use their folder "address" to get papers into their own "houses." They decorated the folders to look like houses.

The children caught on quickly. When one of the folders got out of order, someone always noticed and put it back where it belonged. I only allowed them to file work I wanted them to save. I made the choices. I had everyone file their work from the same activities, things we did that were new, or things that allowed them to be creative, or things they really seemed to enjoy doing. The children liked the idea of saving work in their own folders and I started to think about what I might do next. (Mrs. Avery's story)

Introduction

Student portfolios are gaining acclaim as an assessment strategy from teachers who for years have been saying that "Tests don't show what my students have learned." The literature on educational uses of portfolios covers the gamut from descriptions of how one teacher uses portfolios in a single classroom to reports on portfolios used in high-stakes state assessment programs (Vermont 1991; Mitchell 1992). Portfolios fit the emerging vision of optimally appropriate school practices because of their ability to serve both instructional and assessment purposes. But for someone who has never used portfolios as a student or seen them used in other classrooms, the idea of portfolio assessment may be somewhat mysterious.

What Is a Portfolio?

Asking students to keep a notebook or folder of work over a period of time is not new, but "portfolio" is more than a new name for an old classroom practice. A portfolio is a *purposeful* collection that tells the story of a student's efforts, progress, or achievement in a specified area. From classroom to classroom and situation to situation, the purpose will vary. Sometimes a portfolio is planned to showcase a student's best work and only the "best" pieces are included. Other collections are intended to show growth of knowledge over time, and samples of work from different times of the year are included to document what students can do now that they could not do earlier. Yet other portfolios are planned as learning tools, and there is no intention to use them for assessment.

2

The title of this chapter presents a metaphor for thinking about portfolios. Many teachers are attracted to portfolios as an assessment tool because a focused collection of student work provides more insight into what a child knows and is able to do than most other assessment approaches. Collections give teachers more details about student progress than does daily observation of the students' efforts, using only a grade book to recall what each student accomplished. Examining an entire collection provides more information than considering one piece of work at a time. A mathematician might assert that the whole *is* greater than the sum of the parts, or that keeping a portfolio is like putting ten pounds of potatoes into a five-pound bag.

What does a portfolio look like?

Classroom portfolios can serve many different purposes, and educators are searching for guidelines to help them become aware of the range of possibilities. One of the first matters to consider is, what will a portfolio look like when it is finished? Portfolios take many shapes and forms. Professionals such as artists, architects, or advertising designers typically place their collections in a large leather carrier that enables them to display the many forms and dimensions of their talent and work. Both the visual presentation of the collection (its form and organization) and its contents will influence peoples' judgment about the professional, especially when a job or contract is being offered.

Classroom teachers must be careful to keep the portfolio "product" in proper perspective. The degree to which physical appearance should be a concern will vary depending on the instructional purpose. Simplicity characterizes portfolio use in classrooms where the portfolio is effective. In most cases a simple folder; perhaps a table of contents, a single letter explaining the work, or student comments written on each piece; and the pieces of work themselves are all that is needed. Many teachers use plastic crates and provide each student with a hanging folder where pieces of work are collected. Such informal collections are often referred to as the *working portfolio*. Periodically, the collection will be reviewed and some pieces of work removed. (This procedure is considered in Chapter 2.) At some point the portfolio is put into final form.

3

When the collection is put into its final form, students will typically write a letter or develop an annotated table of contents to explain the significance of the collection and its individual pieces. They might also make decorative folders or arrange the pieces in a particular order to help people appreciate the collection. If the collection was assembled to monitor and evaluate student learning, this final version is typically referred to as the *assessment portfolio.*

Who keeps the collection as it is accumulated?

Students and teachers establish and maintain collections cooperatively. The teacher must provide a place for storing or keeping the collection and should provide sufficiently detailed information about how and if the portfolio will be evaluated. Students are responsible for maintaining the collection and adding pieces, but they should have opportunities to confer with the teacher and their peers when reviewing the collection. More information about the review process is offered in Chapter 2.

Upper-grade students should assume more responsibility for maintaining their own collections. Teachers should periodically remind or give students class time to review their collections and remove pieces that they no longer want to keep. For example, if a student's portfolio contained an assessment that showed the student's ability to use a compass and straight edge to construct angles, then the student made more complex constructions on a later assignment, the student might remove the first paper from the working portfolio because the second one illustrates a higher level of competence. Periodic reviews reduce the number of choices a student must make when it is time to assemble the final portfolio.

What should be put in a portfolio?

The pieces in a portfolio might include class assignments, homework, tests, work completed at learning centers, group projects, journal entries, logs about progress on a major project, drawings, notes from the teacher, and so on. Any student product that documents learning or accomplishment related to the focus of the portfolio is appropriate. Students might include something they did outside of the classroom, perhaps while they were pursuing an outside interest or working in a different teacher's class.

Teachers or students can take photographs of three-dimensional objects or larger pieces of work that do not fit where the collection is kept. One lower-grade teacher asked families to donate a role of film or money toward the cost for developing pictures. After families saw their children's portfolios for the first time, either film or money came from almost every family. Products from group work might also be photographed. An alternative record of group work might be to have students write a paragraph describing their personal contributions to the effort and what they learned from the project. Score sheets or checklists that the teacher used to evaluate a project or an oral presentation could also be included in a portfolio. Printouts from a computer activity and audio or video tapes of student presentations are also appropriate.

When using portfolios in mathematics classrooms, it is important for teachers to carefully plan the *products* of student work. Exciting and challenging class discussions can be a meaningful source of information about what a student knows and is able to do, but the student performance cannot be noted in the portfolio unless some product is produced by the student or the teacher records information in some form. Teachers need to structure discussions and other such activities to ensure that an accurate record of student knowledge and ability is produced for possible inclusion in the portfolio. Some teachers ask students to write about important ideas they remember from a class discussion. Such reflections provide information that is useful, and the writing can then become portfolio pieces.

Should all the pieces in a portfolio be graded by the teacher?

The pieces in a collection do not have to be graded by the teacher before they are selected for inclusion in the portfolio. The student should have some criteria to guide the selection of pieces, but a grade by the teacher is not the only standard that might be used. Some teachers begin using portfolios in their classes by guiding students to include only graded work in the collection. Students soon learn that the portfolio provides the same information as is contained in the teacher's grade book, but the record is far more detailed and interesting.

If the goal of portfolio use is to assess learning that is not considered in other assessment approaches, it would seem that pieces other than graded work should be in the collection. Criteria associated with those other areas of learning should be the focus of student attention in selecting pieces of work to include in the portfolio. Usually a portfolio includes some work that has been graded and some that has not, but teachers may wish to begin with collections of only graded work until they understand how the portfolio will work in their classrooms.

Portfolios: Different Types and Purposes

Portfolios initially came to the attention of school curriculum experts who were in search of ways to assess dimensions of student learning that were not captured by traditional approaches to assessment. Experience with portfolio assessment has also led to an appreciation of the merits of the portfolio as a means of supporting learning, as well as merely assessing it. The literature describing different types of portfolios and their use is perhaps most extensive in the language arts areas, especially the area of writing (Graves and Sunstein 1992; Glazer and Brown 1993). Texts dealing with thematic organization of curriculum featuring integrated or interdisciplinary studies typically recommend the use of portfolios as an assessment tool (Manning, Manning, and Long 1994). The use of portfolios as part of a classroom assessment system is also advocated by early childhood educators (Meisels et al. 1994). The following discussion describes various types of portfolios for mathematics classes.

When trying to identify different types of portfolios, it is necessary to analyze several factors that sometimes overlap. For example, the *showcase* portfolio can be used as an assessment portfolio or not. As a result, the types of portfolios described below are not mutually exclusive. Awareness of the types of portfolios that are used in different contexts is helpful as teachers plan the use of portfolios in their own mathematics classrooms.

Showcase portfolios
When a portfolio contains only the *best* pieces of work related to the areas of learning that are the focus of the collection, it is called a

showcase portfolio. The goal of the showcase approach is to assemble a portfolio containing a limited number of pieces that communicate the student's best accomplishments. Teachers should provide periodic opportunities for students to review their collections and remove work if a similar piece of better quality has been added since the last review. Certain statewide assessment systems use showcase portfolios because it would be impossible to evaluate portfolios from all over the state if each portfolio had a large number of pieces.

In Vermont, for example, the state assessment system for mathematics uses portfolios in combination with other approaches (National Education Goals Panel 1996). The portfolio is designed to assess performance in problem solving and communication, while an "on demand investigation task" and a test in a more traditional format are used to assess other areas of mathematics, such as knowledge of basic concepts, principles, and procedures. A Vermont student's end-of-the-year mathematics portfolio is a showcase portfolio: it contains only five to seven pieces that are selected to document the student's best work related to four problem-solving abilities and three communication skills. These pieces might have been done at any time during the year.

Special uses of showcase portfolios   Problem-solving portfolios and portfolios used to assess communication skills in mathematics are often in a showcase format, especially if the goal is to communicate information about student learning to someone outside the classroom. The "best piece" approach is useful for accountability outside the classroom because student performance on cognitively complex tasks such as problem solving is sometimes inconsistent. In some situations, students' lack of understanding of the context of a problem may impede their success. In other cases, a student may pursue inefficient strategies and get frustrated and not finish a problem. The regular classroom teacher will find observations of such behavior important to guide instructional planning. But when a portfolio is reviewed by professionals outside the classroom, pieces that reflect such behavior are not useful to assess a student's highest level of accomplishment—only samples of "best work" are needed.

Imagine teachers deciding that problem-solving portfolios should be passed on to the next year's teacher each fall. If each student submits a large collection of work, the teachers might be so overwhelmed that none of the work is examined. But a showcase portfolio containing a limited number of pieces can be reviewed easily, and can provide the next teacher with important information that a grade or test score cannot convey. The new teacher will not only see what experiences students have had, but will also learn something about the quality of each student's work and work habits. When teachers in a school initiate a policy of passing portfolios to the next year's teacher, it is important to collaborate in the design of the portfolio requirements. If the portfolios are to be graded or evaluated, teachers need to share the criteria and standards that will be used at different grade levels.

Growth portfolios

One alternative to a showcase portfolio is a *growth portfolio*, which demonstrates the development of knowledge and ability over time. When the goal of a portfolio is to document change or growth, early pieces of work showing errors or exhibiting misunderstandings might be included with later pieces of work to demonstrate improvement. Some teachers encourage students to make corrections or edit papers to show the acquisition of skills.

> Mrs. Davis saw that William's grandmother had already arrived when she entered the conference room with William. Mrs. Conley's eyes twinkled when she looked at her grandson, but her expression tightened as she greeted his teacher. Mrs. Davis reminded herself that it was important to allow the child to explain the portfolio to family members. After greeting Mrs. Conley, she smiled at William, who was awkwardly juggling his folder of work. "What do you have to show your grandmother, William?"
>
> William timidly showed the report he had just written about the product test his group completed last week. He explained to his grandmother, "We asked everybody to taste different brands of popcorn and tell which one they liked best. Then we made a graph about what they said."

8

Picking another two papers from the folder he quickly
said, "This is my seatwork about dividing, and . . ."

His grandmother interrupted, saying, "You have some
x's on there."

William smiled and proudly said, "Yes, but I got to do
'edit' and got all of 'em right. And look at this paper I did
in September. I got mostly x's then. Now I'm only getting
a couple x's sometimes."

As you can see from William's story, a portfolio is a natural
tool for providing a record of progress in learning over time. This
type of portfolio is different from the showcase approach because
it is important to have pieces of work to serve as markers of initial
performance. Some teachers wait a week or so at the beginning
of the school year before explaining the plan for using portfolios;
students then select the work they want to use as their beginning
pieces. These are dated, placed in the collections, and never removed because they show the students' beginning knowledge.
During the year, other papers that show work related to the same
content are added to the collection if they show that learning has
occurred. When a brand new area of work or a new phase of difficulty in study is initiated, teachers might decide that students
should add other papers to the initial group to serve as a basis for
future evaluation of growth.

Other teachers prefer a more formal approach. At the beginning of the school year they conduct preliminary activities and instruction to help learners establish confidence and a comfort level
with classroom routines and expectations. Eventually teachers
give students specific tasks that relate to the areas of learning that
will be the focus of the portfolio. This work becomes the record
of beginning knowledge and ability, and is placed permanently in
the front of the portfolio.

After the initial pieces are identified, the teacher and students collaborate to select pieces that show growth related to the
focus of the portfolio. The contents of the portfolio are reviewed
at regular intervals. The initial pieces are kept, as are one or two
examples of the learner's work in a category; other documents in
that category are removed if the pieces are of better quality. This

procedure controls the amount of documentation in the portfolio and facilitates periodic reflection on learners' progress.

The payoff of keeping a growth portfolio comes when a student, like William, is able to look back at work done two or three months ago and compare it to more recent work. Such reflection on progress is focused on celebrating what has been accomplished, rather than on diagnosing what has not been learned. The effect on a student's motivation, self-confidence, and overall attitude can be remarkable.

Special uses of growth portfolios   The use of a growth portfolio is appropriate any time there is an expectation of continuous growth. Problem solving or communication in mathematics are excellent areas of focus for a growth portfolio. Why would a teacher use a growth portfolio rather than the showcase approach? One of the strengths of the showcase portfolio is its size. If the collection is to be sent out for accountability purposes or is to be passed on from grade to grade, the showcase style is more manageable. If the goal is to plan instruction, to motivate learners, or to report progress to families or to those overseeing programs for special needs learners, the detailed information in a growth portfolio is invaluable.

Some teachers use growth portfolios when students are trying to develop skill with computation. However, except with learners who are having extreme difficulty, this kind of portfolio typically reveals little more than a record of scores would.

An individual growth portfolio would be very useful when working with an especially precocious child. The child might be provided opportunities to study areas beyond typical grade-level content. The portfolio would provide a tool for the teacher to assess the student's progress and serve as a gauge to verify that the child is learning and gaining new insights.

In assessing young children, the strength of the portfolio approach to document change over a period of time is obvious. A young child's knowledge grows so quickly that it is a real challenge to monitor and document the changes that occur. This is especially true of children who come to school less well prepared for academic work. They may learn a great deal and acquire a number of new skills, but still not have the success with school tasks that better-prepared five- or six-year-olds might. If the only index of their growth is performance on things that children of the same age can typically do, such children will always look like unsuccessful learners. A portfolio allows the teacher and others to monitor the real accomplishments of such children. Similarly, the accomplishments of children who always go beyond the expected level of performance can be observed by reviewing growth portfolios they compile.

Those who evaluate curricula or who examine the effectiveness of a particular teaching strategy or instructional approach often look for measures such as *gain scores* from standardized tests to use as a basis for their evaluation. Such indices are often challenged as being inadequate. The portfolio provides an alternative for those who want to target evaluation on areas of learning such as the use of higher-order thinking, problem solving, and the ability to apply mathematics to situations outside of school.

A growth portfolio would also be especially appropriate for students who are in special education programs or who are new to a school system. Teachers usually write a specific set of goals and objectives for each child in special education. Such Individual Educational Program Outlines (IEP) would serve as guides to identify categories of learning or performance that should be documented in student portfolios. The portfolio approach can also be especially useful with students from other countries whose first language is not the language spoken in the school. Examination of such a student's work over time will provide insight into how much English fluency affects the student's performance. The teacher could also monitor development of skill in English. The information that portfolios give the teachers of such children is outweighed in importance only by the effect that such collections have on students. Being evaluated with a system that focuses on how much has been accomplished rather than on how much is left to be learned is highly motivational to students who face unique challenges in school.

Portfolios as an instructional tool

In the vignette in the beginning of this chapter, Mrs. Avery talks about how she initiated portfolio use in her first-grade classroom

11

with an instructional purpose in mind. She wanted the children to learn how to keep and manage a collection so that she could determine if portfolio assessment would work, should she decide to implement it. In her class, portfolio use gave students an opportunity to practice working with "order of numbers" in the context of a meaningful experience. The idea that folder numbers were like street addresses connected the classroom experience to an out-of-school application.

Like Mrs. Avery, many teachers introduce students to the idea of a portfolio without connecting it to assessment. For example, there are certain areas of mathematics, such as geometry or measurement, in which students need to learn a special vocabulary. In such areas the teacher might help students plan a collection of their work that will help them remember details about what they have learned. The instructional value of such a portfolio is that it becomes a student's personal text for quick reference or periodic review of key knowledge.

If students see the collection as a personal study or learning tool, they often work to create outlines or study guides with pictures or diagrams to include in the portfolio. Such student-designed pieces often exceed what a teacher would have expected or required of the student. The student-built collection focuses on content that the *student* sees as important or challenging. It also evolves into a cognitive map of information the student wants to remember, and may help students see new connections and relationships among the things they study.

Before she started to teach measurement, one third-grade teacher, Mrs. Gregory, asked her students to write her a letter telling all they had learned in previous years about the metric system. Carl's response (Figure 1–1) reveals the confusion many children experience when both the English and metric measurement systems are taught.

Mrs. Gregory decided to have students keep a *measurement portfolio.* She commented, "I could have used drill and practice activities to help them identify which units went with which system—and which were for length or liquid and such, but they'd probably forget it and get confused again. I decided to have students save everything we did with measurement. My goal was to eliminate this confusion [about the two systems]."

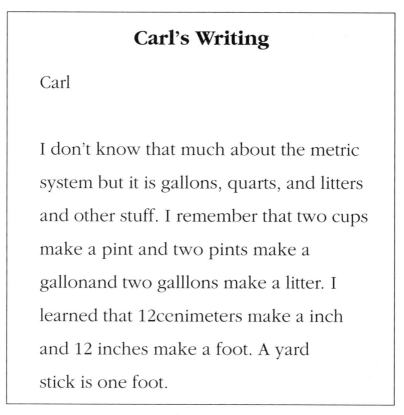

Carl's Writing

Carl

I don't know that much about the metric system but it is gallons, quarts, and litters and other stuff. I remember that two cups make a pint and two pints make a gallonand two galllons make a litter. I learned that 12cenimeters make a inch and 12 inches make a foot. A yard stick is one foot.

Figure 1–1

On the first day, the students made their portfolios. They decorated their file folders and planned tables of contents. Mrs. Gregory guided the discussion. The children thought they would put English-system pieces in the front and metric-system papers in the back. Some children decided to put a piece of art paper in the folder to separate the pieces dealing with the different systems. The teacher suggested that they also try to keep track of how many pieces they had for length, liquid measure, and other subjects, and of which units they had studied. The children decided to make lists of categories and leave blanks to write in the measurement units (Figure 1–2). These lists became guides to the collections.

Measurement Topics for Third Grade Students

Metric	English
Length	Length
_____	_____
_____	_____
_____	_____
_____	_____
Area	Area
_____	_____
_____	_____
_____	_____
Liquid Measure	Liquid Measure
_____	_____
_____	_____
_____	_____

Figure 1–2

When students finished a paper or project dealing with measurement, Mrs. Gregory directed them to put it in their measurement portfolio. She reminded them to label it to match the appropriate category in the table of contents. If the piece of work was about a new measurement unit, that unit name would be added to the list in the table of contents.

The children examined their portfolios periodically. If they had a lot of papers in one category, they selected pieces to save, being sure to keep pieces that dealt with all the different concepts and skills they had studied. In this regard, the portfolio served an additional purpose: learners began to see connections and relate new ideas to previously learned content as they developed the cumulative collection of their work. The periodic review of the contents was important. Suggestions about how to engage students in this review and in discussion of their work are provided in Chapter 2.

Upon hearing about Mrs. Gregory's experience, the other

third-grade teachers in the school decided to have all of their students keep measurement portfolios. They developed an official table of contents based on the objectives for measurement study listed in the district's curriculum guide. They tried to relate each curriculum objective to a title on the table of contents. Some of the teachers gave students the entire table of contents at once. Others gave their students a partial table of contents each report period listing the specific topics to be studied that period. Figure 1–3 shows one page of the table of contents teachers developed. Being

---

Measurement Topics from District Guide

Name _____

Directions: Put two pieces of work for each category.
             Put dates in spaces to show which paper you
             selected.

Topics
Length   Metric   Customary

a. construction of tools   ____ ____ | ____ ____
b. estimation   ____ ____ | ____ ____
c. comparison & order   ____ ____ | ____ ____
d. length, height, width   ____ ____ | ____ ____
e. select unit & tool   ____ ____ | ____ ____
f. scale models
   —with blocks or materials   ____ ____ | ____ ____
   —graph paper or drawings   ____ ____ | ____ ____
g. unit conversion
   within a system   ____ ____ | ____ ____
h. problem-solving situation   ____ ____ | ____ ____

Some thoughts on my work

Things I know I can do.   Things I want to learn.

Figure 1–3

required to respond to the "Things I Can Do" and the "Things I Want to Learn" sections encouraged students to reflect on their learning, on what they had accomplished, and on what they should do next.

Portfolios to support career exploration

In the upper elementary and middle school grades, career exploration is frequently an important part of the school curriculum. This provides mathematics teachers the opportunity to help students learn to "value the role of mathematics in our culture and society" (NCTM 1989, p. 84). Mathematics teachers often invite students to explore work done by people in a particular job or profession and to determine the knowledge and abilities needed for that type of work, giving particular attention to the use of mathematics.

Career exploration portfolios are much like project reports, and often teachers will grade or evaluate the portfolio as they would other types of reports on careers. The important benefit of using a portfolio, rather than a project report, is that the portfolio helps students compile information about careers in light of their own interests and qualifications. As part of the portfolio, students should evaluate their own qualifications for the career they are studying by including documentation of their personal accomplishments, interests, and activities from in-school and out-of-school experiences.

Portfolios for assessing specific areas of student learning

Sometimes the path to a goal is so obvious it becomes invisible. A major goal of the alternative assessment movement as described in the standards adopted by the National Council of Teachers of Mathematics (1989, 1995) is to identify strategies to measure student learning that are more consistent with curriculum goals and with instructional approaches. What better match could there be than to use an assessment approach that focuses on the products of routine instructional activity? If instruction matches curriculum goals and the products of instruction become the tools of assessment, powerful alignment of curriculum, instruction, and assessment occurs.

One of the most common uses of portfolio assessment is to monitor student learning in targeted areas. Frequently a teacher will use the portfolio approach to assess learning in areas that are difficult to monitor with other assessment strategies. For example, development in areas of cognition such as reasoning ability or analytic thinking can be monitored using the portfolio approach, while other methods of assessment often fall short.

The following sections describe the use of portfolios to assess different areas of mathematics learning. Each description states what will be assessed by the portfolio and offers a strategy or outline to be used to guide students in assembling the portfolio. This type of planning is important to the successful use of portfolio assessment. The portfolios discussed in this section are intended as examples. Teachers might use them as models to plan assessment portfolios for other content areas. Also, some of the portfolios discussed earlier in the chapter as serving instructional purposes (e.g., the geometry portfolio and the measurement portfolio) could also be used to assess student learning in those areas. A portfolio designed for instructional purposes can also be used as an assessment portfolio if the teacher designs a set of criteria and standards by which the portfolio is to be judged. Strategies for doing this are in Chapter 3.

Portfolios to assess problem solving   Teachers typically find it easiest to focus on targeted outcomes as they initiate the use of portfolios for assessment. Figure 1–4 is a sample outline that might be used to guide students' decisions about what should be put in a portfolio to demonstrate their problem-solving ability. The relationship between these directions and the criteria for grading the portfolio is explored in Chapter 3. For now, it is sufficient to recognize that decisions about what to include in an assessment portfolio should be guided by a clear vision or plan about the student learning, knowledge, or ability that will be evaluated.

In this example (which is probably appropriate for grades three and higher), four dimensions of problem-solving ability are to be assessed. Students are asked to include pieces of work to demonstrate (1) insight and understanding into the problem, (2) ability to find—and explain their approach to—solutions, (3) use

---

Problem-Solving Portfolio

<u>Directions to student about selecting pieces for the portfolio</u>
Write a sentence for each piece to explain why you decided to include it in the portfolio. The understandings and abilities you are to demonstrate are outlined below.

<u>Insight and Understanding</u>
Select three pieces of work to show you can identify important questions and/or problems in different fields (social studies, art, music, science, mathematics, writing).

<u>Ability to Find Solutions and Communicate</u>
Select three pieces of work to show that you can develop strategies to find answers or solutions to questions or problems. Explain how and why you think the answer is correct.

<u>Basic Skill or Knowledge</u>
Select three pieces of work to show that you know basic information, concepts, procedures, and principles.

<u>Ability to Verify or Validate Solutions</u>
Select three pieces of work to show that you can critically analyze and review your conclusions.

Figure 1–4

of basic skill or knowledge, and (4) ability to verify or validate solutions. Although this portfolio is planned to document mathematics learning, students might include work in other subject areas, classes, and even out-of-school activities that are appropriate to the collection. Students begin to make connections between mathematics and what they study in other fields when work from other subjects is accepted as documentation of mathematics learning in the portfolio.

Portfolios to assess learning during thematic units

Mr. Jackson wasn't sure he wanted to go to the faculty meeting. The principal had asked him to tell the other teachers about the instructional unit he had just finished. It was organized around the theme "the heart." Mr. Jackson didn't know how he would be able to explain to the other teachers how much he thought his fifth graders had learned. If he couldn't do that, he knew he'd never be able to convince them that it was worth all the extra work. As he walked into the meeting with his stack of student portfolios, he could feel the skepticism in the air. He doesn't remember a thing about the faculty meeting until the moment he found himself distributing the portfolios and beginning his explanation.

"You all know I don't like to brag, and I'm never one who looks for extra work. But I was amazed at what happened in my classroom over the past few weeks. I thought I'd let you look at these portfolios instead of giving a speech. Notice in the inside front cover, every student has written a letter telling what they put in the folder and why. They were also supposed to explain what they learned during the unit.

"In P.E. class the students did line dancing and we had them stop three times to take their pulse. I got a kick out of Edward's letter. He included the record sheet from that activity and explained that now he understands why his grandfather yells at him when he tries to hurry along when they are walking somewhere.

"Look at Jenny's folder. She wrote that the only reason she included the report about an animal's heart size was because she had to show she had connected math and science. Most of her pieces are about the love poems she read. I liked her comment that she learned the difference between a 'broken heart' and 'heart disease'—You never know what these kids are thinking!"

Mr. Jackson's use of portfolios occurred in the context of an interdisciplinary unit where the heart was a unifying theme. Those who recommend interdisciplinary studies agree that such

19

an approach to curriculum and instruction should result in unique learning that would not have occurred without the interdisciplinary approach (Tchudi and Lafer 1996; Five and Dionisio 1996). Mr. Jackson's grade book for language arts, mathematics, science, and social studies looked the same as always. He had recorded grades from tests, projects, and assignments in each subject area.

Mr. Jackson's portfolio requirements were designed to assess what students had learned as a result of studying the thematic unit that they would not have learned otherwise (see Figure 1–5). Notice that the initial directions to the students also contain statements about how the portfolio will be evaluated. The students' letters that Mr. Jackson shared were about what they learned and what they saw as important in the unit of study. The contents of the portfolios revealed that the two-week thematic unit resulted in student learning about subject-related knowledge and skills.

Heart Unit Portfolio

Dear Students,

For the next two weeks all of our classes and projects will focus on the theme, "the heart." Each student will develop a portfolio to showcase their ability to relate ideas from different subjects to a study of the heart. When you are finished you will select five pieces of work to show what you have learned about hearts. You must include at least one piece from science and one from mathematics. You will also write a letter to explain what you learned and why you selected the pieces you did.

Very truly yours,
Mr. Jackson

Figure 1–5

The portfolios also demonstrated that attitudes had changed and students had acquired new insights into the importance of healthy habits.

Mr. Jackson could have focused the portfolio to assess other domains. The problem-solving ability outlined in Figure 1–4 might have been adapted to suit the heart unit. But in this case, the teacher wanted to assess the students' ability to make connections and relate ideas that were explored during the thematic unit of study; this portfolio approach helped him do that.

Portfolios to assess all areas studied during a period of time
Some teachers prefer to have students complete a comprehensive portfolio documenting all the topics studied in the mathematics class. The teacher may continue to use traditional tests and graded assignments to monitor some aspects of learning and provide continuous feedback to students. These pieces might be put in the student portfolio. When this approach is used, the teacher provides a checklist or grid specifying the particular areas of learning to be assessed with the portfolio. This helps students determine what types of pieces need to be included in the collection. When using grids, it is helpful for the students to record a code or date on the grid to show which pieces of work match the categories in the grid. It is also helpful to have students write on each peice why it was included.

> Mrs. Sumi wanted to find a way to show students, their parents, and the principal both the breadth of content covered in her sixth-grade classroom and the high levels of success the students had in each area. She decided a portfolio system would serve that purpose.
> "I told the students we would maintain a working portfolio to be sure we were able to put together a complete showcase portfolio at the end of the report period to show parents and other visitors to our classroom. It was their job to keep all the work they did related to the different math topics we'd be studying. I told them we would look over the collection every now and then so they could remove pieces that would not be needed later.
> "I gave the students a grid to keep track of the

21

collection [Figure 1–6]. You can imagine their surprise when they saw the outline of all we planned to do. One student commented, 'I like it better when you make us work without knowing how much we're doing!'

"We went over the first column and I explained that it outlined all the major topics we would be studying. The headings suggested the kinds of pieces they might choose. I told them I hoped they would be able to include at least one of each kind and that they would have to have two pieces of work for each topic. I pointed out to them that some of these, like their investigations or the group inquiry project, would relate to a number of different topics and that they would find the grid format useful to keep track of everything. If they used geometry, fractions, problem-solving strategies, or models in doing one project they would be able to put checks in all the appropriate boxes.

"I also told them that they could include things they did outside of mathematics class if they related to one of the topics we were studying. That strategy ended up being a real surprise for me. Several kids had pieces that showed they saw connections between math class and things they were doing in other subjects. One student brought a project for the portfolio that was completed to earn a scouting badge because, as he said, 'I got to check a lot of boxes with this one!'"

Mrs. Sumi's strategy of having students monitor their collections not only made her job easier, it also resulted in students thinking more about what they were studying. Figure 1–6 illustrates one approach to specifying requirements for a portfolio that covers all the topics studied during a time period. With younger children, a teacher may want to specify particular tasks students should include in the collection, but still require them to check which tasks deal with particular topics. It would also be possible to let students choose the types of pieces to be included, as was done in many of the portfolio models presented earlier in this chapter (see Figure 1–3).

Mrs. Sumi's comment that the final portfolio would be a

Mathematics Portfolio Outline
Second Report Period

Include two pieces of work for each topic. The pieces can be any type.

Topics	Home-work	Quizzes/ Tests	Projects (Group)	Types of work: Investi-gations	Class-work	Other
Fractions and Number Sense						
Fractions and Operations						
Problem Solving						
Relationships: Fractions and Decimals						
Use of Estimation						
Transformation of Geometric Figures						
Congruence and Similarity						
Angle Measure						
Patterns and Problem Solving						
Geometric Models and Problem Solving						
Geometry Outside the Classroom						

Figure 1–6

"showcase" again illustrates that the types of portfolios discussed in this chapter overlap. Showcase portfolios can be graded or ungraded. If they are graded they become assessment portfolios. The working portfolio in Mrs. Sumi's class contained work of mixed quality. When students finalized the portfolio at the end of the report period, their task would be to identify the best pieces associated with the topics on the outline to include in their final showcase portfolio.

Using a portfolio to assess everything that is covered during a period of time is somewhat more cumbersome than using portfolios to target specific areas, but the overall portfolio has several benefits. A *comprehensive portfolio* can present a broad and dynamic picture of a student's learning. It can cover areas of learning that may also be assessed in other ways. This type of portfolio will often contain graded papers such as tests, homework, or class assignments; the teacher may or may not have already recorded those scores in a grade book. When graded papers are included, it is common for teachers to encourage students to edit them. Thus, the inclusion of graded papers lets students show improvement or additional learning. They may revise a paper, correct errors in exercises or problems, or completely redo a task to demonstrate that they have acquired the knowledge and ability they did not have when the original task was completed.

Because of its breadth, a comprehensive portfolio can be an excellent tool for instructional planning. The portfolio gives the teacher a summative picture of a student's learning. It showcases areas where the student is most successful and accomplished and informs about early difficulties that have or have not been overcome. And it vividly reveals dimensions of knowledge or performance that do not meet expected standards. The overall portfolio becomes an especially rich tool for successful and meaningful conferences with students and families as well.

Portfolios to assess young children
Teachers in the early grades (Martin 1994) and others who use a curriculum approach that emphasizes the integration of subject matter or a whole language philosophy find that portfolio assessment fits naturally into their classrooms. They often like the comprehensive approach because they are not artificially forced to

associate each piece of work with a particular school subject. The same is true when considering portfolio use for young children. In most cases a targeted approach is a good starting place, but a teacher may want to focus the portfolio on the child's social development or acquisition of general growth as a learner, rather than connecting the portfolio with only one school subject.

Nationally, there has been a movement to thoroughly and carefully monitor many aspects of learning, growth, and development in young children. The portfolio is recognized as an assessment approach that is especially appropriate when working with children in preschool and primary grades. Early childhood educators are aware of the dramatic changes that occur within a short time as children come to school. Keeping actual samples of work to share with parents provides a meaningful way of communicating what the child knows and is able to do.

Sometimes it is difficult to store the pieces that young children produce. One kindergarten teacher uses a large pizza box for each child's work. These are stacked in the corners of the room. Other teachers use photos to keep records of any work that cannot be kept in the children's folders. When working with a child whose writing skills have not developed sufficiently, the teacher or an aide can ask the child to talk about a drawing they might have done to represent a mathematical idea. The adult can then write what the child says on the piece before it is put into the portfolio.

First- or second-grade children's responses to open-ended questions often provide interesting pieces to include in a mathematics portfolio. Asking children on the twenty-fifth day of school to record all the different ways they could use coins to make twenty-five cents, on the fiftieth day of school to make fifty cents, and on the hundredth day of school to make a dollar provides pieces that show the progression of a child's ability to work with money. Perhaps the most interesting part of these pieces, however, is that they show the development of children's ability to record and communicate their responses.

Evidence of learning, especially in very young children, can be subtle. In some cases a child's success with a particular task is inconsistent. The seeming success of today disappears tomorrow. In other cases, knowledge or ability that was demonstrated in one context seems to disappear when a related task calls for use of that same understanding or skill. On the positive side, a child often has that "a-ha" experience, when ideas somehow magically come together and what seemed like a formidable learning goal yesterday can suddenly be accomplished with ease.

The Work Sampling System (Meisels et al. 1994) was developed to continuously monitor progress from preschool (three-year-olds) through elementary school. A portfolio is only one part of the documentation used in this system. The benefits of such a comprehensive assessment system are explored in a later chapter. The Work Sampling System illustrates the potential of portfolio use with very young children, especially when the goal is to document change over time.

Portfolios: Some Other Benefits

If one of the goals of mathematics learning is for students to see connections in what they study, it becomes important for them to remember what came before today's lesson. Often when someone asks children what they did in math class today the answer is "nothing." Teachers who ask students what they did yesterday often get the same response. The tasks in a mathematics class are treated like hurdles that students jump over and leave behind. The collection of work in a portfolio could become a reference when students don't remember working on something that was taught last week, and can help them to make connections between things they study.

Keeping a portfolio also affects student motivation. Teachers sometimes complain that students are too "grade conscious," caring more about their grades or scores than about the quality of their work or how much they have learned. This behavior is not really surprising, in light of the way students are evaluated. After student work is graded in a traditional classroom, the paper is returned and only the grade or score is kept. If a student wishes to discuss a report card grade later in the semester, it is the record of scores in the teacher's grade book that is the focus of conversation. Apparently the grade is all one needs to think about to understand how well a student is doing! The use of portfolios transmits a different message. Conversations about success with learning are connected to instructional tasks, and the student work, not the grade, is what seems to be important.

When students maintain a collection of their work, a valuable message is communicated. The message is that there is something about the pieces in the collection that is more important than the grade earned or the score the teacher assigned. The act of reviewing the pieces periodically reinforces that message. Having students actually examine pieces of work, some of which may not have been graded by the teacher, to select the best pieces also directs attention to what has been learned and diminishes the importance of the number or letter the teacher wrote at the top of the page. Other aspects of the process of keeping a portfolio are discussed in Chapter 2.

Summary

The fabric of school experience is woven from a variety of events, tasks, and interactions, any of which can serve different purposes on different occasions. For example, a student project assignment might be intended to guide students' search for information, to challenge students to reconcile inconsistencies in their understanding of concepts, or to provide the teacher with information about what each student does or does not know about a topic.

The alignment of curriculum, instruction, and assessment poses one of two strong arguments for portfolio assessment. Indeed, the fabric of school experience is even more tightly woven when the products of classroom activity in a portfolio become the basis for assessing student learning. The second argument for using portfolio assessment deals with the failure of many assessment approaches to provide accurate indices of learning in certain areas. The portfolio is an excellent way to monitor change over time in these and other areas.

This chapter suggests approaches that teachers might use to experiment with portfolios in their classrooms and answers questions that are commonly asked by those thinking about portfolios for the first time. A teacher's short-term experience using portfolios in ways similar to those described in this chapter may provide experience that will lead to success with more complex future use of portfolio assessment.

Simplicity is a key to the successful use of portfolios. High levels of student responsibility and careful planning by the teacher will lead to new partnerships that support student learning. The simple, focused collection of student work becomes like ten pounds of potatoes in a five-pound bag: you get more than you expect from such a simple package.

Chapter 2

A Portfolio Culture: Classroom Procedures

The students were absorbed in their conversations and didn't even notice Mrs. Carnes, the principal, enter the third-grade classroom. Harold rolled his eyes and squirmed as his teacher suggested that Mrs. Carnes sit with his group. After greeting the students, Mrs. Carnes asked Harold to talk about what they were doing. He began, "Well, everybody needs help to decide what to put in their portfolio. Everybody is looking at someone's and talking about it and asking questions."

Mrs. Carnes said, "Oh, I see, why don't you continue what you were doing and I will ask if I don't understand. Or you can ask me, if I could help."

After a moment Lonzena said, "Okay, we were talking about the papers we did on multiplication. I don't know which one to pick. What are you putting in?"

Marcia said, "I put in one of my homework papers from the book. I got them all right and there were a lot of them."

"Is that what we are supposed to write on our entry sheet where it says 'why you picked this one'?" Phil interrupted.

Harold answered, "Sure, unless you have a better reason for picking it."

Lonzena asked again, "What did you use for multiplication, Harold?"

Harold responded, "I think I'll use the paper we did last Friday. It has those two story problems at the end that are always hard to do and I got 'em right. And I only missed one other one when I said two times three is five. I'm always doin' something dumb like that but this time I only did it once."

"I have the same trouble," Lonzena commented. "Every paper has mistakes on it. I just can't find one to use. I could use the problem solving one we did last week but I used the calculator and I want some paper to show I *can* multiply."

Marcia looked over Lonzena's papers and suggested, "Maybe you should ask Mrs. Granby if you can edit one of your papers. Remember, she said that we could do that if we wanted to show we know how to do it now, even though we got some wrong when we did a paper."

Phil said, "Yeah, find one where you won't have to do too many so it won't be too hard to do and you can say that you like how you can make corrections in the second part of the entry sheet."

Introduction

The type of conversation Mrs. Carnes observed becomes a natural part of the discourse in classrooms where portfolio assessment is used. The students were engaged in discussions about the work they did, how well they did it, their strengths, and what they were finding difficult. Such conversations represent important changes in the roles students assume in the classroom where teachers are using portfolios.

Mrs. Granby's students made several references to the "entry sheet." When selecting pieces of work for the final assessment portfolio, they completed this sheet (Figure 2–1) to explain why each piece of work was an important part of the collection. Such rationale statements are typically required when students are keeping a portfolio for assessment purposes.

To complete such a sheet, students must know the criteria that will be used to judge their work. They must also learn to reflect on the quality of their work in light of those criteria. This chapter discusses the portfolio process, showing how it affects different teachers' classrooms, and suggests strategies to facilitate the effective use

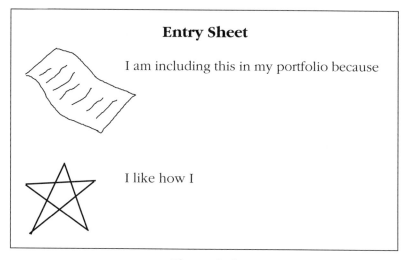

Figure 2–1

of portfolios. This chapter also addresses the question of how students can successfully become involved in the portfolio process.

Changes in the Culture of the Classroom

Spandel and Culham (1994) refer to what they call a "portfolio culture" to describe how classrooms change when portfolios are used effectively (see Figure 2–2). In a portfolio culture the roles of students and teachers are reshaped. Students participate in setting goals and planning activities. They actively monitor their own learning, rather than merely "receiving" instruction. Both teacher and student have a voice in deciding what the student knows and is able to do and what topics need additional work. Such student involvement is the focus of reports that claim that the portfolio process is more important than the product itself.

The Changing Roles of Teachers and Students

Recent literature on assessment (Neill et al. 1995) details the changing role of students in the assessment of their classroom accomplishments and their learning. Research and teachers' experiences

31

Characteristics of a Portfolio Culture

(from: Vicki Spandel and Ruth Culham, "Creating the Portfolio," a workshop handout copyright by Northwest Regional Education Laboratory, Portland, OR)

1. Students help to set their own goals/plan their own activities.
2. Thinking skills are valued and taught.
3. Not everything gets assessed.
4. Students take an active role in learning.
5. Diverse responses/solutions are sought and valued.
6. Teachers view themselves as coaches/mentors.
7. Learning is valued more than perfect performance.

Figure 2–2

are providing substantial support for assessment procedures that involve a great deal of student self-appraisal and reflection. Although the ultimate evaluation decision may still be the responsibility of the teacher, the teacher is no longer seen as the purveyor of information, the director of inquisition, and the judge of adequacy. Rather, the teacher becomes a facilitator and a coach or mentor. As teachers accept this new vision of their role, they must find ways to modify their instructional practices.

Teacher as facilitator

As a facilitator, the teacher provides experiences and opportunities that will capture student interest in what is to be learned according to the school curriculum. This is accomplished by allowing students to address personal interests, emphasizing dimensions of the topic or extending their study beyond the scope of what is traditionally taught at that level of schooling. One approach to this is the inquiry cycle described by Short and her colleagues (Short et al. 1996). Use of the inquiry cycle enables the class, small groups of students, or individuals to explore a topic, formulate their own questions, and pursue answers as part of their class work. Teachers and students negotiate to define questions that are consistent with the school curriculum, the teacher's views about what should be studied, and the students' interests.

The Project Learning approach (Katz and Chard 1994) allows students in large or small groups to study a single topic in depth. This approach has been initiated in early childhood settings. It requires that the teacher guide children carefully without dampening their curiosity and enthusiasm. The common strategies used in models where the teacher acts as a facilitator are

- beginning instruction based on what students know
- helping students identify questions or share what they wonder about
- guiding students as they search for information or gather data related to their questions
- allowing students to share what they have learned
- encouraging students to formulate new questions or search for extensions of what they have learned

This approach to teaching is challenging and requires that the teacher be aware of individual interests. The teacher can help students focus their inquiry in ways that complement the goals of the regular curriculum.

Katz and Chard suggest not that the project approach should supplant all other instruction, but that it might allow students to extend concepts they have studied or pursue at greater depth ideas they learned as part of the regular program of instruction. In a mathematics class there will of course be times when teachers explain, demonstrate, or model procedures that students need to learn. However, it is most effective if these demonstrations occur because the learners need to know how to do something to fulfill their own purposes or pursue their own inquiry. In other cases students may attempt to use the mathematics they learn in an applied setting that interests them.

Assessing learning when students are given such independence might seem difficult. The portfolio becomes an excellent tool, for it enables students to submit pieces that are both personally meaningful and related to the expected learning goals. The teacher facilitates students' demonstration of knowledge and ability by defining broad guidelines or specific requirements that will guide students to demonstrate learning that fits the school curriculum, as well as other areas of learning that the student sees as important or interesting.

Teacher as coach

A teacher who assumes the role of coach or mentor faces several challenges. First, the teacher must find strategies to help students learn how to learn. A common approach to this is to give students tasks or pose questions that are open ended. The teacher must be careful not to give too many specific directions about how to pursue the task or too many hints about how to answer the question—that would spoil the inquiry experience. Confronting ambiguity typically increases students' anxiety. This is where the teacher puts on the coach hat.

> "Mrs. Murray, you asked us to work out a plan to decide where we should go for our class field trip. We decided we'd have a class meeting, have students nominate places, and then we'll take a vote. The highest vote says where we'll go. Is that all you want us to do?"
>
> Mrs. Murray smiled and began, "Veronica, that plan might work. What kind of places does your group think students might pick?"
>
> David responded, "Not the zoo or the museum, we've been there before."
>
> Julie suggested, "I'd pick the mill. We go by it every day and I always wonder what goes on in there."
>
> "They won't let kids in there," Robin interrupted. "I know 'cause my dad works there. I think we should go someplace neat. I'd like to go to Disney World."
>
> Veronica exclaimed, "Oh, that's ridiculous, do you know how far away that is? We'd have to go on an airplane—stay overnight. I don't think the school would pay for that and I'm not sure my mom would let me go."
>
> As the student conversation ebbed, Mrs. Murray commented, "You've brought up some interesting points. What is it that you have to consider in order to plan the field trip?"
>
> Jack responded, "I guess we have to worry about

how much it will cost, how far away it is, and if the kids would have fun on the trip—and stuff like that."

"Okay," said Mrs. Murray, "I'll let you work on that for a while. You might want to think about the information you will need before we decide on a place. Also think about how you will get that information."

Mrs. Murray was able to help her students determine what they needed to do to complete an assigned task by asking questions. Some students find it frustrating when teachers respond to their questions with more questions, but teachers who want to focus on higher-order thinking must acquire good questioning strategies (Harris Freedman 1994).

The portfolio documentation of this activity might be a description of procedures, decisions about what to do next, and eventual findings. Sometimes students like to put this in the form of a job log, where the names of the students who are responsible for certain work are also listed. Other teachers ask individual students to write a description of how their group tackled the problem and what they decided.

Students' new roles

The use of such questioning strategies not only changes the teacher's instructional approach, it also prepares students to assume a greater role in the evaluation process. As long as teachers respond to students by saying "That's right," "Good job," "You're finished," and "Next, you need to . . . ," students will avoid reviewing their own work. When their responsibility and independence as learners are encouraged, students learn that *they* must figure out when the job is done, and done well. Students will start to review their work in a different way if they are responsible for defining the task that's needed to accomplish a goal rather than merely following the teacher's directions. Evaluation of the work on such an assignment would consider both how the student completed the task and the quality of the final product. As students develop the ability to reflect on their work to determine when they are finished and how well they have done, teachers develop confidence in the students' judgments about what they know, what they need to learn, and what should be done to accomplish that learning.

Changes in Curriculum and Instruction

When teachers use an assessment tool that provides the opportunity to monitor more than routine, factual knowledge, they become more aware of their students' broader intellectual potential. In a classroom where traditional curriculum and instructional approaches are used, portfolio use may reveal that the scope of activity offered to students is narrow. It doesn't make sense to have students keep portfolios if the only pieces they have to include are test papers and routine textbook-based tasks and assignments. If that is all that is available, the portfolio becomes a very fat grade book, and no true insight is gained from the contents. Portfolio use is appropriate only if the teacher can identify something that the student will learn, or that the teacher will learn about the student from the portfolio.

Teachers who are committed to portfolio use begin to look for new curriculum materials and new tasks for students. When using these materials, they soon realize that portfolios are more interesting and assess different dimensions of student performance when they include students' responses to complex tasks that involve higher-order thinking. Because portfolios provide a framework to examine more sophisticated dimensions of learning, the teacher is apt to continue the search for new materials. In short, the curriculum of the classroom is enhanced, as is discussed further in Chapter 5.

This new version of classroom teaching and learning has many benefits. As students take an increased responsibility for judgments about their learning, they acquire important skills that will help them become independent learners, an ability that will support their success when they make the eventual transition from school to the workplace.

The Portfolio Process

The literature on portfolio use repeatedly emphasizes the portfolio as a process. Those who use portfolios successfully have integrated the process into their teaching so thoroughly that, as Spandel and Culham (1994) say, a new culture emerges. The portfolio process involves students in six phases of activity that truly reshape life in the classroom.

1. Students learn about the purpose of the portfolio and the criteria that will be the basis for assessment. Ideally, the students participate in determining those criteria.
2. Students review their collections periodically. The work they do is not put aside and forgotten once it is completed and graded by the teacher.
3. Students participate in selecting pieces for the portfolio. It is the student's responsibility to identify the pieces that match the evaluation criteria.
4. Students reflect on their accomplishments and set goals for future learning.
5. Students are more closely involved in a cooperative, rather than competitive, relationship with their peers.
6. Students have opportunities to comment on the significance or meaning of their collections. These comments are typically communicated in a variety of forms and to a number of different individuals.

In order for students to participate in these activities, they must learn to be reflective and honest at each stage of the process. If portfolio use is to be effective, teachers must help students develop the ability to examine and critique their own work. The following sections discuss each phase of the portfolio process, highlighting the kind of student reflection that is involved at that stage.

Reflection: Learning what to consider
In many classrooms, evaluation criteria seem to be a secret that teachers keep from students. Statements such as, "The teacher *gave* me a B," or questions such as, "Why did *you take off* three points," suggest that students have little understanding of the basis for evaluation decisions. The teacher's expectations seem like a mystery, or a target that students must hit while blindfolded. Clearly this is not always the case, but students especially feel it is true when the tasks given allow them to be creative, to make interpretations, or to use alternative approaches. Students find such ambiguous tasks frustrating because they have a sense that there is some "right" way to proceed and they see the task as a game to find that right way. One of the first steps in implementing portfolio

use is to demystify evaluation criteria and standards of performance. The class meeting approach is a good way to begin, even
in primary grades.

> All eyes shifted to Mr. Edwards as he moved the easel to
> the center of the room and said it was time for another
> class meeting. The students knew that their comments
> were going to be written on the easel. They had done this
> before when they decided on class rules.
>
> Mr. Edwards started by reminding them of the activity
> they had done last week with two-color counters. They
> had tried to find all the combinations of red and yellow
> they could make using five counters (for example, two
> red and three yellow). Mark blurted out, "I got more than
> anybody else 'cause I didn't pay attention to repeats!"
>
> "That's right, Mark," Mr. Edwards responded. "Today
> we're going to do the same thing, but this time I'm going
> to ask you to do it using *nine* counters. But before you
> begin, let's talk about what we should look for to tell
> whether or not you did a good job."
>
> Clariss said, "I think it's good if you get a lot of them.
> Maybe we should try to see how many we can get."
>
> Mark interrupted, "But you can't have repeats unless
> they're the backwards ones, you know, where the num-
> bers are switched."
>
> "It's important to be neat and to draw pictures to
> show what you mean. . . ."
>
> As the discussion continued, Mr. Edwards printed on
> the easel to record the things students agreed were im-
> portant to pay attention to when doing their work. The
> children decided that they would
>
> * get as many combinations as possible
> * not have repeats
> * have pictures for each combination
> * write correct number sentences with each picture

Mr. Edwards' use of a class meeting was an excellent way to
help students learn about what was expected. Making this kind of

discussion a part of classroom routine creates a context for student participation in the portfolio process. The more frequently such discussions occur, the less time they will take, and the more attuned students will be to assessing the quality of their own work in light of meaningful criteria. The goal then is to develop the learner's concept of "quality work."

Students are apt to have considerable difficulty the first time a teacher asks them, "How do you know when your work is quality work?" They will not be able to identify observable characteristics or features that they can use to evaluate their work. Students who have never had the opportunity to critique and evaluate their own work or the work of peers typically will produce two types of responses. First, they will look to an external expert to provide the decision, saying such things as, "The teacher said it was good," or "There are no x's, I got them *all* right." Then, when pushed for further responses, students typically comment on the process they underwent in doing the work. Answers such as, "I worked really hard," "I checked my work," and "I was careful" show an understanding of good work habits, but are not useful in evaluating final products.

In the case of Mr. Edwards' class, students were able to generate criteria for quality work on the task with nine counters because they had previous experience with the task with five counters. They had a concrete basis to use as they explored their ideas about what characteristics would define quality work on the task. They had done the task before, and knew the expectations for performance and the pitfalls.

Teachers will find that students are often preoccupied with criteria such as neatness and accuracy if most of their mathematics work has dealt with computation where neatness, speed, and accuracy were praised by adults. A teacher may want to initiate class discussions about quality when considering tasks that are open ended and provide an opportunity for diverse responses. Eventually, students may be able to identify generic characteristics of quality work in mathematics, such as

- explanations are clear
- diagrams or drawings are provided
- important labels are included on pictures and diagrams
- work is legible

39

- good strategies are used
- more than one solution strategy is shown
- why the answer made sense is explained
- the discussion includes ways to extend (or apply) what was found

This list will vary, of course, with different age levels, and some of the items may not fit all the kinds of mathematics work a student may do at a particular time. Students should be invited to add items to their list of characteristics of quality work as they think of them. It is helpful to talk about which characteristics might apply when students begin work on a new task.

Routine classroom activities can also provide a context for learning about the characteristics of quality work. Using writing as a tool to enhance mathematics learning is receiving increased attention (Stenmark 1989; Whitin, Mills, and O'Keefe 1990). A good follow-up activity for a writing assignment is to have students meet in small groups and read each other's work. As the students discuss the written pieces, the teacher might ask them to list things that make one piece of writing "better" than another. Students might generate a list of characteristics of quality writing about mathematics. These would become criteria for evaluation and would be hints each student could use to guide future work. Students will notice things such as

- If you're telling someone how to do something, it's important to put things in a special order.
- It's good to give examples to show what you are talking about.
- Sometimes it is helpful to draw a picture.
- You should try to spell math terms correctly.
- You might want to explain what you mean when you use a special term.

Each time a new type of activity is presented for the first time, a teacher will find it is useful to have some discussion about what constitutes "quality work" for this kind of assignment. Eventually students will learn to think about criteria each time they do an assignment. This would be an important development in any classroom, but in one where portfolios are used, learning the criteria for quality is an essential skill.

Reflection and self-evaluation: Learning to look back

The expression "beauty is in the eye of the beholder" is true even in the face of existing definitions of beauty. Even though students may be aware of criteria for judging quality, it takes some practice to learn to apply the criteria to the products of one's own labor. One fifth-grade teacher's approach to portfolio assessment shows how a teacher can help students develop the habit of looking over past work and being honest in the review.

The students were to save pieces of work in a working portfolio from which they would eventually select pieces for a show-case portfolio for each report card period. The teacher told them they could only select pieces of work that she had graded (Figure 2–3). Students were reminded to look over their collections periodically. The teacher initially gave class time to allow students to work in groups to discuss the pieces they were saving. She eventually stopped allocating class time for this activity and required that it be done during the time they had each day for independent work.

The teacher explained that students' collections would be recognized as "blue ribbon" or "red ribbon" portfolios if they met the required standard. A blue ribbon portfolio had to contain at least ten pieces that were graded A, while a red ribbon portfolio had to have at least ten pieces that were graded either A or B. The teacher did not build the rating of the portfolio into the report card grade because all of the work in the portfolio had been graded and was already recorded in the teacher's grade book, which was the basis for the report card grade.

At the end of the report period, the students had to narrow their collections to fifteen pieces of work, three in each category. The teacher encouraged the students to talk about the pieces they had selected and about the things they had done well. They could describe their collection as being a blue ribbon or red ribbon portfolio, or, if they had not met the standard, they would discuss the portfolio as a collection of the best work for the period.

This teacher's use of a portfolio represents a modest first

Showcase Portfolio Outline

Student Name _____

Title of Work   Date   Grade

<u>Mathematics</u>

_____ _____ _____
_____ _____ _____
_____ _____ _____

<u>Language Arts/Writing</u>

_____ _____ _____
_____ _____ _____
_____ _____ _____

<u>Language Arts/Other Areas</u>

_____ _____ _____
_____ _____ _____
_____ _____ _____

<u>Science</u>

_____ _____ _____
_____ _____ _____
_____ _____ _____

<u>Social Studies</u>

_____ _____ _____
_____ _____ _____
_____ _____ _____

Figure 2–3

attempt that controlled both the amount of teacher work and the amount of class time required to keep the portfolios. Yet these collections had several important positive effects on students. First, although most of the student reflection was focused on the grades they got on the pieces, it did encourage students to think about how well they were doing. Second, the standard for ribbon recognition was attainable for all students. The final portfolio contained fifteen pieces of work, and red ribbons were awarded to any student who had B or better grades on ten pieces. Because of the range of difficulty in assignments during the period, it was possible for every child to get a red ribbon or a blue ribbon if they truly worked toward that goal The teacher reported one student's request that they get another mathematics assignment because, "I only need one more A to have a blue ribbon collection."

Graded assignments and homework take on new significance for the child who is doing a piece of work thinking about the need for a good paper for the portfolio. Consideration of low-achieving students' approach to daily work suggests that they may not recognize daily or routine classroom activity as important to their learning. When pieces of daily work are potential entries for the showcase portfolio, students come to see that daily work is important. In this way the portfolio process can guide learners to be more effective students as they start paying attention to all opportunities to learn.

Although it may seem frivolous to allocate time for students to review their collections and add or delete pieces, it is time well spent. The focus of the review might at first be to create a "blue ribbon" portfolio. But students will learn about looking back over their accomplishments. Students should eventually be expected to look back over ungraded work in light of the criteria that will be used for evaluation or in light of their personal goals for learning.

Reflection and self-evaluation: Learning to select pieces

When students were selecting the pieces to use in the portfolios to earn red or blue ribbons, they experienced the responsibility of examining their own work to pick the best pieces. This was not a challenging task because they were reviewing only graded papers and they did not truly have to compare individual pieces of work to assess quality. A strategy that helps students learn to examine their own work in light of learning goals is to organize the collection around specific knowledge or abilities identified in the mathematics curriculum. Figure 2–4 shows an outline a teacher might use to guide a collection of work related to a unit of study on quantitative literacy. The portfolio outline is not a list of activities done in class, but, rather, the objectives for the unit of study. The categories on the portfolio outline sheet specifically identify what

Quantitative Literacy
Portfolio Outline

Student Name _____

Dates

Strategies used to explore

(a) experiments or simulations   _____ _____

(b) technology   _____ _____

(c) use of books, magazines, newspapers, . . ._____ _____

(d) data collection and management   _____ _____

Communication of information

(e) make graphs, tables, charts   _____ _____

(f) explain information contained on
    graphs, tables, charts   _____ _____

Thinking, Reasoning, Applying Knowledge

(g) make inferences or predictions based
    on data   _____ _____

(h) evaluate conclusions, inferences,
    or predictions   _____ _____

(i) connect concepts of probability or
    statistics to study in other fields.   _____ _____

**You are to include one or two pieces of work to
document performance in each area.**

Figure 2–4

students should know and be able to do after the unit of study. It is likely that the teacher provided a number of experiences for students related to each objective. This outline was developed for use in a middle school setting, but with revision it might be suitable for several different grade levels.

In order to select pieces, students must learn to look at their work in light of the instructional objectives. They must be in tune with what they are supposed to be learning. When a teacher provides several activities related to each of the areas on the outline, students have choices about which piece demonstrates their best work in each category. In some cases, the inclusion of a single major project or report might provide evidence related to several categories on the outline. A student's decision to use one piece to cover several categories would reveal that the student has learned to examine assignments in light of the goals of instruction and the criteria for quality work.

Many teachers find it convenient to have students write a statement about each piece of work as it is completed, either on the back of the piece itself or on an attached sheet (Figure 1–2). Students are asked to write about things such as "what you learned while doing the task," or "what the class was studying," or "anything you want to remember about doing this paper." Student responses will include statements such as "This is about adding more than two numbers," or "I learned how to use the computer to make a circle graph when we did this project," or "I thought this was hard to do and had to get help." Such notes are very helpful when a student is reviewing work or selecting pieces for the final assessment portfolio. Having students write statements about what they learned while doing a paper also helps them develop the habit of thinking about their work in terms of learning goals.

> Mrs. Hampton joined a group of students who were discussing the final selection of pieces for the portfolios they would show their families at the Spring Open House. Deborah looked puzzled as she asked Roger why he had decided to include the test paper where his grade was B. She inquired, "Some of your other papers on that topic are better—look, you didn't make any mistakes on that one. Why don't you select it for your portfolio?"

Roger sighed and responded, "I was having a lot of trouble with those problems. My dad helped me three nights in a row. When I told him I got a B on the test he got Popsicles for all of us. I'll never forget how good it was to have the whole family celebrate for me! Do you think it's okay to put this one in, Mrs. Hampton?"

As Mrs. Hampton looked through the papers Roger had selected, she responded, "Deborah, you have a good point. Students do want to be sure to select papers showing that they can do each thing we studied. Roger, you have a different reason for wanting to include this piece and it is a good one. You need to write an explanation about the piece in your opening letter to say you made fewer mistakes on other papers but this is one that makes you proud because of how hard you worked to understand the procedures you used. It is a good idea to include pieces of work that you are proud of—even if the score isn't perfect. This paper shows you are persistent, even when you find things are hard."

Two important principles are illustrated by this interaction. First, the importance of a cooperative environment where peers can assist one another in reviewing portfolios is obvious. This aspect of the portfolio process is discussed later.

Second, a student's choice of what to include may hold some surprises. Students may not select the same pieces the teacher would for the final collection. In some cases, this occurs because students don't understand the criteria or the knowledge they are to document. In others, students may not be examining their work carefully, leading to random selections. In still others, a student like Roger may have a reason that is not related to the portfolio guidelines but is a matter of great personal importance. It is important to respect such choices, but to help the student offer a rationale for the selection that will ensure appropriate evaluation of the portfolio.

Guiding or interfering with student choices   Students are asked to provide an explanation of why they selected particular pieces to be in the collection. When the portfolio is going to be made public, or graded, or passed on to next year's teacher, it is important to communicate the basis of student choice. Because the selection of a piece might result in inappropriate documentation of learning, the grade or the inferences made by others about the student's accomplishments would be incorrect if the rationale for the selection is not clear.

Student rationale statements often reveal a great deal about the learner and suggest strategies or approaches to support future learning. For example, Roger might have selected the paper he did because it was one that he found difficult to do and, having finished it, he felt a great sense of accomplishment. Or perhaps he wanted to include it because of his memory about working with his father and the family celebration. Knowing that the paper revealed difficult areas for Roger, the teacher might want to provide additional experiences to reinforce what he had struggled to understand. The rationale statement that explains pride in the accomplishment also communicates that the student really wants to share that piece with a parent at the school-family conference.

Recognizing the significance and meaning of student choices is important as teachers guide the completion of students' final portfolios. The teacher must either help the student reconsider the selections or, in some cases, suggest what information should be included in a rationale statement to ensure that those who are making judgments about the student based on the portfolio will understand the significance of each piece. Sometimes it is necessary to explicitly suggest that students include different pieces than those selected. This could be done by saying, "I am not sure this is the piece you want to include, I'd like you to look over all of your work and think about . . ."

Some teachers encourage students to include a few pieces that are personally meaningful. A student might pick the piece that was the most challenging, the most interesting, or the most fun to do. Having a section of such "mosts" adds dimension to a collection and helps the portfolio capture the personal side of the learning story.

Reflection and self-evaluation: Setting goals for the future
As the portfolio process is put into place in a classroom, students develop a surprisingly sophisticated understanding of where they are going in mathematics. As students become aware of assessment

criteria and learn to look at their own work in light of those criteria, they can set a course for their future work. Asking students to identify personal goals for learning is a natural next step in the portfolio process. This can be done as part of a conversation with the teacher. The goals could be put in writing as a part of the completed portfolio itself, or they could be communicated during a school-family conference where the student is a participant.

Mrs. Roberts went to Duncan's desk and asked him to show her the pieces he had selected for the showcase portfolio. Duncan began, "This is the one I did using the newspaper. Remember, we had to find one thing that was advertised by different stores and figure out the differences in price. I found three stores that were having a sale on shoes like mine. The most expensive was five dollars more than the other two."

Mrs. Roberts responded, "That seems like a good choice for the portfolio. Be sure to write an explanation of why you selected that piece. Tell me about why you included this multiplication paper."

Duncan commented, "I'm really having trouble with that. I worked with John and corrected the ones I got wrong, but I'm still having trouble with multiplying on other papers. This is the best one I have for multiplication."

The teacher asked, "Duncan, why do you think you are having trouble with this?"

"Oh, I don't know," Duncan responded.

"Now, this was a homework paper. Do you do better on class assignments or on homework papers?" the teacher asked.

"Well, I don't know. My mom keeps telling me I'm always too much in a hurry to get things done at home. But I guess I just don't know the multiplication facts yet," Duncan responded.

The teacher suggested, "Have you thought about listing something about multiplication in your goals for the next nine weeks?"

"Yes," Duncan responded, "I wrote that I want to get better at multiplying."

"Did you list some things you want to do to improve?" the teacher asked.

Duncan thought a moment and said, "I didn't write that part yet. Maybe I can try to do my math assignment when I first get home. There's nothing good on TV then and it would be easier to think about it."

"Okay, what else might help?" asked the teacher.

After a few moments Duncan responded, "I guess I should use the flash cards and play that math game at the learning center. You told me to do that, but I like going to the reading corner. I guess I really need to get to know the multiplication facts better."

"Those are good ideas," replied the teacher. "Are there any other goals or things you want to work on?"

The reflection and goal-setting part of the portfolio is sometimes the most important part. Again, this will be difficult for students at first, and they are apt to focus on areas where they will really be able to see their progress, such as computation. The teacher may prompt the students to include goals that may be hard for them to state. For example, students might need to work on making estimates of length, or remembering characteristics of geometric shapes, or identifying the question in a problem-solving situation. The main purpose of this goal-setting activity is to help students focus on what they need to know. Also, helping them identify the strategies they can use gives students a plan to follow to reach their goals.

Reflection and self-evaluation: Benefits of a cooperative classroom

Encouraging peer support during the portfolio review process is beneficial in a number of ways. The first, but perhaps the least significant, is efficiency. If a teacher tried to have a separate conversation with every student about the selection of each piece of work, a great deal of valuable time would be lost. Many of the decisions about the collection are routine and teacher guidance is not really needed. Yet it is helpful for students to have someone to consult during the process of selecting pieces. Many times students can answer each other's questions about format or about whether a particular paper fits a certain category in the portfolio outline. Without such peer assistance, the process of putting the final portfolio together could become very frustrating. Working with peers and not having to check every detail with the teacher helps students develop confidence. It also makes the process more manageable for the teacher.

As students talk about their collections and share ideas, they will also develop an independence that will be important for future academic success. Students learn from looking at other people's work. Even students who usually have perfect papers will benefit from seeing how others organize information, how they record procedures, and how people use different strategies to solve a problem. When students have opportunities to see the kind of work others do, they have models for improving themselves. After listening to groups of students talk about one another's work, one teacher reminisced about her own elementary school experience.

> I can remember how envious I was of one of my friends in third grade who could use crayons in ways that made her work gorgeous. Each time we used crayons I would watch the colors she chose, how she used light and dark shading, everything! I kept trying to master the techniques she used to improve my own work.
>
> You know today, as I listened to my students discuss their papers, I realized they were doing the same thing. Each person was trying to find out how the way others did their work might "fit" into their own plan to do better in math class.

Reflection and self-evaluation: Making conclusions public

Occasions when students share their portfolios with those outside the classroom provide opportunities for affirmation and celebration. But how can parents, principals, and others outside the classroom understand portfolios? Effective strategies must be employed to help the outside audience understand the portfolio's purpose and significance. Students will be encouraged and proud when the response of those who see their collections is supportive. In short, the sharing of an assessment portfolio with an outside audience is an important part of the portfolio process.

The context and rituals associated with making portfolios public can vary considerably. The dynamics of the situation depend on who is present and what is to be accomplished. Many teachers have found parent conferences to be a perfect occasion for sharing student portfolios. In fact, the term "school-family conference" more appropriately describes these events because typically the student is present and plays a critical role in the meeting. The student presents the portfolio and explains the work that was selected for the collection. It is important, however, for students to know what is expected of them at such a meeting. One fourth-grade teacher employs strategies that help both the student and the family prepare for the school-family conference. After students have selected the work to include in their portfolios, they complete an evaluation of their work on a form that also includes a place for the teacher's remarks and a place for a family member's comments (see Figure 2–5).

Family members are invited to come to the conference fifteen minutes before the meeting with the teacher. When they arrive they have an opportunity to examine the portfolio and the teacher's and student's remarks about the collection of work. Students know that their family members will look at the folders before the conference and will see what the teacher and student thought about the work before completing the "Family Comments" section. When it is time for the meeting, the teacher, family members, and the student participate in the conversation. The student can have a meaningful role at the conference because the discussion is about the collection of work and the goals the student has set.

> Mr. Heard greeted Mrs. Graham and she looked up from Gloria's portfolio. "Hello, it is good to see you, Mrs. Graham, and I am so glad Gloria could come as well." Joining the pair at the table, Mr. Heard suggested that Gloria should begin by telling her grandmother about the work in the folder, and why she had selected those pieces. Gloria started.

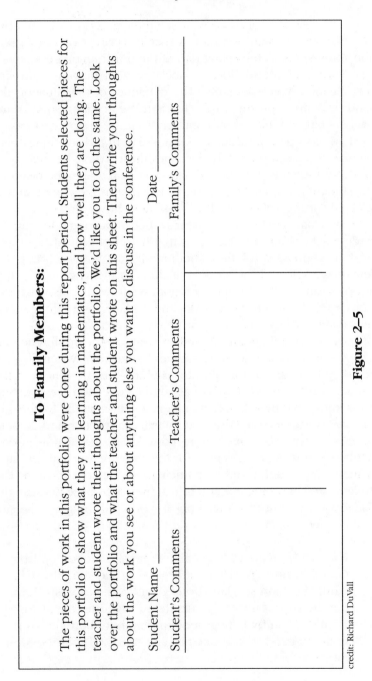

To Family Members:

The pieces of work in this portfolio were done during this report period. Students selected pieces for this portfolio to show what they are learning in mathematics, and how well they are doing. The teacher and student wrote their thoughts about the portfolio. We'd like you to do the same. Look over the portfolio and what the teacher and student wrote on this sheet. Then write your thoughts about the work you see or about anything else you want to discuss in the conference.

Student Name _____   Date _____

Student's Comments   Teacher's Comments   Family's Comments

Figure 2–5

"We have to have three pieces of work from math, language arts, science, and social studies. I picked these math papers because Mr. Heard told us to pick pieces we thought were interesting and pieces that showed our best work. Remember, last year—I was having a lot of trouble with division and I kept bringing home papers with mistakes I had to correct—finally I think I caught on—so I put this paper in the portfolio so you could see that I can do it now. I thought this activity with pattern blocks was really interesting. After we made a design, Mr. Heard told us the green triangles cost five cents. I had to figure out how many green triangles it would take to cover my pictures and that told me how much the design would cost."

A fourth-grade student couldn't speak as Gloria did without some preparation. The students in Mr. Heard's class were accustomed to discussing their work with one another. They also had practiced what they might say at the conference to explain their portfolios to family members. Such practice activities are more than mere rehearsals. When students talk about their work with peers, they see the strategies other students use to approach academic tasks and they learn language they might want to use in talking about their own portfolios.

Many students will also gain recognition for their academic accomplishments while showing others their portfolio pieces. Occasions for recognition of academic performance are typically formal events such as spelling bees, "academic bowls," or other contests that are only available to a few exceptional students. Portfolio discussion sessions allow all learners to show their accomplishments. In some way the presentations of portfolios are like intramurals sports, in which all students can participate and just about everyone makes a "play" that causes others to cheer.

Summary

This chapter focuses on the portfolio process. The change that occurs in the culture of the classroom offers one of the most compelling arguments for using portfolios. The kind of responsibility students assume in that process becomes a learning experience in itself. The concept of shared responsibility in the assessment of learning, which is part of the portfolio process, creates teacher-student partnerships and encourages cooperation among peers. It is clear that the portfolio process supports the development of skills that are essential for tomorrow's citizens.

It is also important to note the partnerships that form outside the classroom. A teacher's conversations with a learner's family no longer focus on scores, grades, and other abstractions. The communication with family members, next year's teacher, or others is brought to a very concrete level when the actual work students do is the focus of conversation.

This chapter describes the successes of teachers who use portfolio assessment in various ways. The portfolio process is a developmental one that provides opportunities for students to learn academic content and intellectual behaviors that many students do not typically acquire. It is important to remember how the use of portfolio assessment can affect classroom practices and rituals in positive ways. Transforming to a portfolio culture indeed makes portfolio use manageable for the teacher and a growth experience for students.

Chapter 3

Portfolio Evaluation and Grading: What Should I Do with This Pile of Papers?

Frank Clayborn heaved a sigh as James Robinson came into the teachers' work room. He had been plodding through the portfolios from his pre-algebra class and was feeling like the task would never end. Frank confided, "This is the first time in years I've had the feeling that I don't know what on earth I'm doing! These portfolios were great. My students really got into doing them, and thinking about their work, and setting goals, and all that stuff you read about in the journals. Now I have to grade the things and I'm not at all sure how to do it!"

James chuckled, "I had the same trouble the first time I tried portfolios. Why not give everybody a 'pass' and get yourself off the hook?"

Shaking his head, Frank scowled, "It seems like that would be defeating my whole purpose for doing these! Is that what you do with yours?"

"No, the first time I did portfolios I had an afternoon just like the one you're having and then I hit upon this idea that I'd write down just a few things to pay attention to as I graded them."

Introduction

The conversation between Frank Clayborn and James Robinson highlights the usefulness of making a distinction between "assessment" and "evaluation" (Chittenden 1991). As teachers begin to use alternative assessment approaches such as portfolios, they often find it helpful to reflect on the difference. Some authors treat these terms as synonymous, but this chapter makes a distinction between the terms. "Assessment" refers to *gathering information.* Thus "alternative assessment strategies" suggest different ways teachers use to elicit, or gather, desired information about student learning. "Evaluation" is used as a label for *the act of making judgments* about student learning based on inferences about the assessment data.

Frank had an *assessment* plan that guided his students to gather information that documented what they knew and were able to do. He may have planned and carefully implemented one of the approaches suggested in Chapter 1 of this book. When his students submitted their portfolios, he faced the question of how to *evaluate* them. How should he decide that this student should be directed to do further work related to an area being studied, while that one should be told to move on to new challenges? How should he determine that this student will get an A or a certain number of points, while that student will get a C or fewer points?

There is no one best way to do the evaluation, just as there is no one best way to gather the information. There are, however, some inappropriate ways or inappropriate practices that provide inaccurate records of student knowledge, ability, and accomplishment, thus defeating the purpose of using alternative assessment strategies. In short, some strategies provide a better index of student learning than others. This chapter describes and explores approaches that can be used to evaluate student portfolios. Key questions asked by teachers implementing portfolio assessment are addressed: Is it always necessary to grade portfolios? If you do grade them, when should the evaluation be made, and by whom? How do you judge collections and communicate the basis of your evaluation decisions to parents and others outside the classroom?

What Is a Rubric?

Recent literature on assessment uses the term *rubric* to describe a key concept in the evaluation process. A rubric is nothing more than a system or specification of rules to evaluate student work. In truth, teachers have always used rubrics in grading papers. Consider the different ways teachers might evaluate the student responses in Figure 3–1.

A very simple rubric that teachers commonly use is: the answer must be completely accurate and have a label to be correct. If the answer is inaccurate or the label is missing, the answer is wrong. Using this rule, Melanie's answer would be marked correct and all the other students' answers would be marked wrong: Jeffrey did not include the "cm" label; Jodie measured the table and desk incorrectly, and the numerical part of her answer was not accurate; Harry made a subtraction error. Notice that this rubric identifies two characteristics of performance to be considered in grading. An answer must have both the numerical part and a unit-of-measurement label to be correct.

Another teacher's rubric might not require a label. Because that rule would only focus on the accuracy of the answer, both Jeffrey's and Melanie's answers would be correct. Jodie's answer

---

Student Responses

Task:

How much higher is the teacher's desk than your group's table?

Melanie's Paper		Jeffrey's Paper	
Teacher's Desk	76 cm	Teacher's Desk	76
Our Table	−64 cm	Our Table	−64
	12 cm		12
Jodie's Paper		Harry's Paper	
Teacher's Desk	53 cm	Teacher's Desk	76
Our Table	−23 cm	Our Table	−64
	30 cm		22 cm

Figure 3–1

would be wrong even though the subtraction was correct, because the wrong measurements were used.

Another teacher might say that both characteristics of the answer are equally important and award partial credit if only one part is correct. Melanie's answer should get two points, while Jeffrey's would get only one point because he forgot the label.

Yet another teacher might want to consider a third characteristic of performance and give credit for measuring the objects correctly, doing the calculation, and using a label. This teacher's rubric would result in three points for Melanie; two points for Jeffrey; two points for Harry, who measured correctly and labeled the answer, but subtracted incorrectly; and two points for Jodie, who subtracted correctly and labeled the answer, but used the wrong measurements in the first place.

The purpose here is not to rationalize or debate these teachers' different approaches to grading or their decisions about what they wanted to evaluate. The point is that evaluation that involves more than a "right answer" approach requires guidelines to govern scoring. If the criteria, or focus, of the evaluation are not specifically defined and made known to students, the teacher's subjectivity may be questioned. Teachers have traditionally used such scoring schemes, but not expressed them as formal written rubrics. As *assessment* approaches become more sophisticated and complex, written guidelines for the *evaluation* of student work are needed. Hence the rubrics have become an important part of professional discussions.

A central message of Chapter 1 is that a portfolio is a collection made with a particular purpose in mind. If that purpose is to evaluate learning, a rubric is needed to identify the criteria or characteristics of the work that will be examined to determine the grade. The rubric used to evaluate a portfolio is the public statement of the specific knowledge, skills, and understandings that should be documented in the portfolio.

In the anecdote at the beginning of this chapter, Robinson advised Clayborn to "write down just a few things to pay attention to." Developing a rubric to guide the grading of portfolios is nothing more than explicitly writing what will be considered in determining a score or grade. Formulating such an explicit statement can ensure fairness and consistency and take the mystery and subjectivity out of the evaluation process. Evaluating responses to open-ended questions, portfolios, and other performance tasks becomes more objective when an explicit rubric is used.

Different types of rubrics

The literature on assessment describes different scoring approaches guided by different types of rubrics (Kuhs 1994). The *holistic scoring approach* commonly used in the assessment of student writing is often difficult for teachers to implement. A truly holistic approach does not identify particular characteristics that are defined separately and explicitly in the rubric. Rather, student papers that have been completed and evaluated are used to define the levels in the rubric. These work samples, called *anchor papers*, are the standard of expected performance at each level and are models of student work that communicate the essence of the various levels of performance in the rubric. Any piece of work is judged by the degree to which it matches the anchor papers at a particular level. In other words, when a pure holistic scoring approach is used, a decision that a student paper would be graded as a "3" is based on the judgment that it looks like every other "3." This type of rubric is especially useful when evaluating creativity, elegance, and other characteristics of student work that cannot be clearly defined. It is sometimes difficult for a teacher to use a holistic approach when first beginning to work with alternative assessments. For classroom-based assessment in mathematics, it is often useful to use other types of rubrics.

This chapter explores two scoring approaches, *focused holistic* (Charles, Lester, and O'Daffer 1987) and *analytic* (Stenmark 1991). These two approaches were selected for this discussion because they are well suited to mathematics, and those who are learning about rubrics for the first time will have little difficulty developing their own analytic or focused holistic rubrics.

> Mrs. Williams' fifth-grade class had just completed an independent writing task. She had asked each student to write a letter to Jessie, who was absent, explaining how they had learned to add fractions that day. Groups of children were sharing their letters and trying to pick one that would really help Jessie do the assigned exercises.

59

Raymond's group had just selected his letter as the one that should be sent to Jessie. Mrs. Williams asked, "Why did you select Raymond's letter? Why would his be helpful to Jessie?"

"He used the same math words we did in class, like 'numerator' and stuff, but he always explained what the words meant," Amy commented.

Tom interrupted, "And he gave an example every time so you could follow the words. I never thought of doing that."

Valerie added, "I liked the way his letter told you what to do first, second, and stuff. You could really follow the letter and get it done."

Developing a rubric: Dimensions of performance

These children's remarks show how learners can identify characteristics of their work that might be considered in evaluation. Involvement in such discussion is recommended in Chapter 2 as a strategy to help take the secrecy out of evaluation. Such discussions can identify *dimensions* or *characteristics of performance* that can be used as the foundation for either a focused holistic rubric or an analytic rubric.

If Mrs. Williams had her students keep a portfolio of work to show how well they could communicate mathematical ideas or information, she would probably design a rubric that considered the same things that the students thought made Raymond's letter a good one. The dimensions of performance in the rubric might include

- appropriate use of mathematics terms and symbols
- quality of explanations
- use of examples or illustrations
- organization of discussion

Identifying such dimensions of performance is the first step in developing a scoring rubric.

When trying to identify dimensions of performance, the teacher must consult and consider a number of different sources of information. Examining curriculum guides, reflecting on instructional events, observing students as they work, and listening to students' conversations about their work will identify those things that need to be considered in evaluating student work. Just as Mrs. Williams' class was able to identify what made one student's letter to Jessie better than another's, students can describe the things they find challenging or what they feel is important in broader areas of learning.

When developing a rubric to evaluate performance on a single task, teachers often find it useful to actually do the task themselves. As teachers coach students in the early review of their working portfolios, ideas about the things to incorporate in the rubric emerge. Teachers should tell students as much about the rubric as early as possible, but when doing portfolios for the first time the teacher might begin with a simple list and add more details to the list of things to be considered periodically.

Developing a rubric: Which type of scoring?

The selection of a particular scoring approach is a matter of preference, and the decision is usually based on the intended use. The primary difference between a focused holistic rubric and an analytic rubric is that a focused holistic approach results in the designation of a single score for the work being evaluated, while an analytic rubric defines separate scores for each different dimension of performance. If information about student learning is to be used to plan future instruction, a teacher might find the analytic approach more helpful. A simple review of the analytic scores of all the students would identify the areas where student performance is already strong and the areas in which the students need continuing development. On the other hand, if scores will be used only to calculate a report card grade, a teacher would probably find the single score from a focused holistic rubric sufficient. Examples of focused holistic and analytic rubrics are given in the following sections.

Developing a rubric: Selecting a scale

The teacher must also decide how many levels will be useful in designing a rubric. Teachers whose students are highly grade conscious find that using a three-, four-, or six-point scale has

61

several advantages. For each of these there is no obvious connection between the rubric and letter grades A, B, C, D, and F. Students seem to be more open to reflection and more accurate in critiquing their work when their responses don't automatically connect to particular grades used on report cards. Using a three-point scale at the outset is often desirable because the scale is less precise than one with more levels. The teacher does not have to make subtle distinctions in evaluating the work when the rubric is less precise.

A particular three-point scale can also be useful when working with a portfolio that is designed to show change over time. Teachers who want to use a scale that recognizes development or growth over time might use a label or title, instead of a number for each level of the rubric. A publication by teachers in the Ann Arbor public schools (1993) suggests that the labels "not understanding," "developing understanding," and "understanding/applying" can be used to simplify evaluation. Developmental continuums like this are frequently used to evaluate students in primary grades, but would also be appropriate to evaluate a portfolio targeting the learning of complex areas, such as problem solving, communication, and the like. Such a developmental continuum can be very useful for evaluating a portfolio that is reviewed regularly. These labels might also be useful in coaching students on selecting which pieces of work they will include in their portfolios.

Developing a rubric: Standards of performance
Once a decision is made about which type of rubric will be used and what dimensions of performance will be considered, the next and perhaps most difficult decision must be made. *Standards* are established as descriptions of each level in the rubric are written. The teacher and student may have agreed that "use of mathematical terms and symbols" should be considered in determining the grade, but questions such as how many terms, which symbols, etc., are needed to get the highest level on the rubric remain to be defined. What results in decisions that student work should be graded at one level or another? Specifying a standard of performance for each dimension to be evaluated is an important part of writing an evaluation rubric.

Sample Rubrics for Evaluating Individual Pieces of Work

The dimensions of performance suggested earlier for assessing communication in mathematics can be used as the basis for a rubric to evaluate the development of communication ability. Four performance dimensions were suggested as possible indices of students' mathematical communication ability. Students' ability to communicate might be evaluated considering

- appropriate use of mathematics terms and symbols
- quality of explanations
- use of examples or illustrations
- organization of discussion

An analytic rubric would provide guidelines for evaluating performance in each of these four areas, resulting in four separate scores. Figure 3–2 presents an analytic rubric for communication in mathematics based on a three-point scale. The statements at each level are descriptions of an expected standard of performance for students in each category.

Notice that the highest level of performance, level 3, allows for occasional random error. Statements such as "inaccuracies are rare" or "most of the time" are important in designing rubrics for portfolio assessment. Often a student's best and most insightful piece of work is one that contains a random error or oversight. In making a collection, many teachers prefer to encourage students to focus on the depth and scope of their work rather than the fine details and perfection in each piece. Teachers who want to stress the importance of perfection, accuracy, and attention to detail can do this when grading individual assignments. Usually, in portfolio assessment, teachers gain more insight into student learning when there is license to include some pieces of work that have a few flaws. Thus the standard in the rubric is described to allow minor mistakes at high levels in the evaluation scheme.

Other teachers prefer to set a standard that the highest-level score will only be given to portfolios that contain accurate, error-free work. This judgment is influenced by many factors. The teacher's professional convictions, the types of students in the

Three-Point Analytic Rubric Communication in Mathematics

	Not Yet (1)	Developing (2)	Accomplished (3)
Appropriate use of mathematics terms and symbols	Uses everyday words instead of math terms/ symbols or uses incorrect terms or symbols.	Often uses math terms/ symbols, could use more. May sometimes use incorrect term or symbol.	Consistently uses math terms/symbols in oral and written work. In- accurate use is rare.
Quality of explanations	Explanations are inaccurate or unclear.	Explanations are often accurate but may be somewhat unclear or incomplete.	Explanations are com- prehensive and clear. Inaccuracies are rare.
Use of examples or illustrations	Rarely uses examples/ illustrations or those used do not match the idea being discussed.	Some use of examples/ illustrations. Those used may sometimes be con- fusing, unnecessary, or inaccurate.	Regularly offers examples or illustra- tions that enhance communication. Inaccurate or incorrect illustrations are rare.
Organization	The order of discussion is confusing. One idea does not necessarily follow another.	Communication is some- what muddled. More than one idea is discussed simultaneously or the ideas do not flow.	Communication follows a logical sequence most of the time.

Figure 3–2

class, the goals of the curriculum, and the focus of the assessment can all be offered to support one point of view or the other.

Experience with using a rubric to grade individual papers can be helpful to understand how a rubric works when evaluating portfolios. Three fifth-grade students' descriptions of the procedures they followed and the answers they found during a cooperative group activity are presented below. The students were asked to find the perimeter and area of the floor of the classroom and the room's volume. The reader may wish to try to use the rubric in Figure 3–2 to "score" these papers before reading the discussion of each piece.

Tommy's paper (Figure 3–3) has both strengths and weaknesses. His use of terms and symbols does not show full understanding. He labeled area and volume as "inches" instead of "square inches" and "cubic inches." We might say his use of terms is "developing." The explanations seemed incomplete because he did not give the measurements for the length and width of the room or tell how the group calculated the area and volume. Thus

---

Tommy's Writing

First we measured the perimeter of the classroom. It measured 1,218 inches. We used one yard stick and a twelve inch ruler. Then we measured the width of the room. It measured 102 inches. Then we found out the area. It was 80, 275 inches. Then the volume. It was 97, 774, 950 inches. It was fun and exciting. Volume is the amount of space in a room. Perimeter is the outside rim. Area is the amount of space on the floor.

Figure 3–3

a score of "Developing" might also be appropriate for the "quality of explanation" category. He did illustrate the terms by describing perimeter as "the outside rim," area as "the amount of space on the floor," and volume as "the amount of space in the room," so we might decide to say his "use of illustrations" is "accomplished." Some teachers would require a stronger example or illustration to assign the highest score. However, the definitions seem to be an afterthought, so a rating of "developing" might be designated for "organization." Recognizing that this was the first task the class had dealing with all three concepts in one activity, Tommy's paper could be scored as a 2-2-3-2. The numeric codes might be used to keep a record in the teacher's grade book: 3 for

---

Pat's Writing

This is what I know about perimeter. I know that perimeter is the rim or outer edge of something (1,218 inches). I know that area is length times width (80, 275 square inches). I also know that volume is the length times the width times the height of an object (97, 774, 950 inches).

This is how we did it for the volume. We measured up to the ceiling. Then we measured the width and the length of the room.

This is how we did it for perimeter. We measured the rim or outer edge of the room.

This is how we did it for area. We measured the length and width of the room.

Figure 3–4

"accomplished," 2 for "developing," and 1 for "not yet." If this had been a higher grade level, or a task completed later in the school year, the rubric may have imposed a more rigorous set of standards.

Pat's paper (Figure 3–4) exhibits a smooth use of terminology (width, length, square inches) and only the labeling of volume is inaccurate. Pat describes the algorithms used to find area and volume, but when describing how the group found the answer, she only tells about the measuring and does not connect it to the algorithm. Neither does the paper offer illustrations of what area or volume means. The communication might be enhanced if the piece were reorganized. A teacher scoring this paper might conclude that the use of terms and symbols is "accomplished" and all other categories are "developing," and record the score in the grade book as 3-2-2-2.

Meredith's response (Figure 3–5) shows another aspect of

Meredith's Writing

This is what I know about perimeter, volume and area. Perimeter is the edge or rim of something. Volume is the length times the width. Area is the length times the width times the height.

This is the way we did our project. We took a meter stick and a ruler and started measuring around the room for perimeter in inches. Then took the same materials and put it against the wall from top to bottom for volume. Then took the same materials and measured from side to side both ways for length and width. Then added all the inches up and got 97, 774, 950.

Figure 3–5

evaluating a student's work with a rubric. The rubric was developed to assess communication ability, yet it is hard to think about the communication ability in this response because there are so many errors in the content of the writing. The statement about measuring inches with a meter stick and mixing the formulas for area and volume results in a score of 1 for "use of terminology" and 1 for the "quality of explanation." Meredith's explanations are clear, but they are mostly inaccurate, so "quality of explanation" would be evaluated as "not yet" (1). It is hard to think about a score for use of illustrations on Meredith's paper because she illustrated procedures that no other student did (measuring "around the room," "against the wall from top to bottom," and "side to side both ways"). A score of 2 for illustrations might be assigned to recognize this element of Meredith's communication skill. This would not be done if the illustrations were completely inaccurate or were misleading. It is also hard to think about "organization" when inaccuracies break the flow of ideas. Some teachers might say that Meredith's response is as organized as the others and score it 2, while others would say the response is "confusing" and score it 1.

When disagreements about scoring are frequent, it is time to revise the rubric. If more than one person is using the rubric, there should be discussions when such ambiguity arises. A more clearly defined description of the standard, and perhaps a change in the label, may be needed to eliminate such ambiguity in scoring. Sometimes it is even necessary to add a dimension of performance when the rubric is to be used in the future. If the rubric is not revised when such ill-defined choices are identified, grading becomes subjective. No one can ensure that everyone is using the rubric in the same way and holding students to the same standards. It is especially important to revise the rubric if more than one person is using it to score student work.

Communication skills in mathematics might also be evaluated using a focused holistic rubric in which a single score is assigned focusing on several dimensions of performance (Charles, Lester, and O'Daffer 1987). The rubric in Figure 3–6 is based on the same performance dimensions as the analytic rubric in Figure 3–2: use of mathematical terms and symbols, clarity of explana-

---

Focused Holistic Rubric
Communication in Mathematics

Accomplished (3)	—Consistently uses mathematics terms and symbols with few inaccuracies. —Presents comprehensive and clear explanations using examples or illustrations when appropriate. —Offers discussion in an organized and logical sequence.
Developing (2)	—Uses math terms and symbols most of the time but some are inaccurate or incorrect. —Offers correct explanations but statements are unclear or incomplete and examples are either missing or are incorrect. —Responses may be somewhat disorganized.
Not Yet (1)	—Uses terms and symbols incorrectly or relies on everyday words instead of math terminology. —Explanations and examples are incorrect or not relevant. —Order of discussion may be confusing.

Figure 3–6

tions, use of examples or illustrations, and organization. This rubric would probably suit several different grade levels. Upper grade levels would, of course, have more complex writing tasks and more extensive mathematics content to discuss in their writing.

It is sometimes difficult to write a rubric that combines so many performance dimensions. Experience with this rubric revealed that in some cases a student can offer a clear description without using drawings or illustrations. Thus the descriptions of the levels combined those two characteristics in ways that suggested students could use either one or both approaches (that is, a clear explanation, examples or illustrations, or a combination of the two). You may want to evaluate the writing by Tommy, Pat, and Meredith using the rubric in Figure 3–6 before reading the discussion that follows.

Applying the focused holistic rubric to Tommy's, Pat's, and Meredith's papers will reveal some differences between analytic and focused holistic rubrics. You will find that Tommy's and Pat's work would be scored at the "developing" level and that nothing in the record will recognize Tommy's strength in illustrating ideas and Pat's fluency with terminology. Meredith used terms incorrectly, gave incorrect examples, and suggested the measures should all be "added up" to get volume. The discussion would be confusing and misleading to someone who tried to follow the directions on Meredith's paper. The paper would be evaluated as "not yet."

When using a holistic rubric, rather than an analytic one, less information about student learning is communicated by the score. It is also true that using a rubric that has fewer levels (e.g., three rather than five) means that a teacher has fewer distinctions to make when evaluating student work, but it also means a loss of precision in the assigned score. The work that is evaluated at a given level may fit the description of that level, but may have strengths or weaknesses that other papers graded at that level don't.

Expanding a rubric to six levels instead of a three can be done gradually. Initially, level 3 becomes level 6, and level 2 becomes level 4. Level 5 is defined as "better than level 4 but not as good as level 6." Level 1 becomes level 2, and the new level 3 is defined as "better than level 2 but not as good as level 4." Level 1 would indicate that an assignment is incomplete or totally incorrect. Some teachers like to code such assignments as level 0. In such cases they use a six-point scale, 0 to 5 . After having experience with the kind of work that is evaluated as level 5 or level 3, teachers might be able to revise the rubric to explicitly define the kind of work that fits the new levels.

Rubrics for Portfolios

A portfolio outline like those suggested in Chapter 1 often identifies dimensions of performance that may be used in the rubric. For example, Figure 1–4 shows an outline that students were to follow in selecting pieces of work for their problem-solving portfolios. The outline directs students to select pieces to demonstrate learning in four categories:

- insight and understanding into problems
- ability to find solutions and validate the answer
- basic mathematics skill or knowledge
- ability to communicate how the strategies were used and support the approach

These categories could be used as the dimensions of performance for evaluating the portfolio. Thus, in the example in Chapter 1, each student's problem-solving portfolio might receive four scores: one for insight and understanding, one for finding and validating solutions, one for basic knowledge and skill in mathematics, and one for ability to describe and defend the strategies used to solve problems.

Figure 3–7 shows an analytic rubric that would match these performance dimensions. As you examine the various levels in each category you will see that there is a need to make fine distinctions. For example, the evaluation of ability to find solutions and validate answers actually incorporates two different performances; the difference between level 3 and level 2 is that performance in both areas is demonstrated to earn a 3, but a level 2 score might be caused by inadequate demonstration of one area or the other.

A rubric to evaluate individual pieces of work might set higher standards than a portfolio rubric, with minor errors preventing an individual piece of work from getting the highest score. A rubric to evaluate portfolios is typically less demanding. The collection of work in a portfolio is intended to demonstrate what the student knows and is able to do. If the portfolio is to effectively demonstrate a student's ability to solve complex problems or apply mathematics to unfamiliar situations, teachers

Analytic Rubric for Problem-Solving Portfolio

Insight and Understanding

Level 3 Work shows clear understanding of the problem and insight into the importance of information that is given.

Level 2 Work shows understanding of the problem and what needs to be found but insight is weak. The student may misuse or ignore given information that is important or may use information that is extraneous.

Level 1 Work shows little understanding of what the problem is asking and important information is ignored or used inappropriately.

Ability to Find Solutions and Validate the Answer

Level 3 Work shows the ability to select appropriate strategies to work toward a solution (even though occasional computational errors may occur) and student checks work or writes a rationale that explains how the answer "fits" the conditions.

Level 2 Either an inappropriate strategy is selected or the student does not check work and justify the answer in light of the context.

Level 1 Student selects inappropriate strategies and does not check work or discuss the validity of the answer.

Basic Mathematics Skill or Knowledge

Level 3 Correct interpretation of mathematics terms is apparent and computational errors are rare and have been edited.

Level 2 Frequent computational errors, most of which have been edited, or selections do not show knowledge of mathematical terms.

Level 1 Frequent mathematical errors that have not been edited or have been incorrectly edited.

Figure 3–7

Ability to Communicate Explanations of Strategies or Approaches

Level 3 Some work shows ability to explain the procedures that were used and provide a rationale for the decision to use these procedures.

Level 2 Student offers explanations of the procedure used and the rationale for this choice of the approach but the explanation is vague and may have minor errors.

Level 1 Student work does not demonstrate use of communication skills related to procedures and rationale or those that are presented are incorrect and difficult to follow.

Figure 3–7 *Continued*

would want the portfolio grade to be an index of that performance, and would not assign a lower score because of random computational errors.

A rubric that demands perfection will encourage students to select pieces of work that are less complex, because it focuses on computational accuracy as the essential characteristic of a good collection. Allowing students to edit papers when they prepare their final portfolios for evaluation lets them include whatever pieces they feel best represent their problem-solving ability. The edits will also demonstrate the students' ability to find and correct their own errors.

Figure 3–8 shows a focused holistic rubric for a problem-solving portfolio. Five characteristics of student performance are to be considered:

- interpretation of the problem situation
- use of given information
- selection of solution strategies
- mathematical accuracy
- review of answers

Focused Holistic Rubric
to Evaluate Problem-Solving Portfolios

Level 4

The portfolio contains pieces that show:

—accurate interpretation of problem situations or statements most of the time,

—appropriate use of given information,

—use of appropriate strategies that logically relate to the problems,

—only rare or insignificant errors in mathematical procedures,

—evidence that answers were reviewed and evaluated in the context of what they would mean in the given problem situations.

<u>One</u> of the following characteristics distinguishes the Level 4 portfolio:

a) Evidence of creative or insightful, but atypical, approaches to problems,

b) use of technology in either the presentation or solution of a problem,

c) Perseverance and tenacity in dealing with complexity, obscurity, or ambiguity.

Level 3

The portfolio contains pieces that show:

—accurate interpretation of problem situations or statements most of the time,

—appropriate use of given information,

—use of strategies or approaches that logically relate to the problems most of the time,

—few mathematical or procedural errors,

—evidence that answers were usually evaluated in the context of given problems.

Figure 3–8

Level 2
The portfolio contains pieces that show:
— accurate interpretation of problem situations or
statements most of the time, but given information
<u>may</u> be used incorrectly,
— strategies or approaches that logically relate to the
problems are not always used,
— errors in computation or basic procedures may be
common,
— answers seem not to have been evaluated in the
context of the given problem situations.

Level 1
The portfolio contains several pieces that show:
— inaccurate interpretation of problem situations
or statements, or incorrect use of given
information,
— strategies or approaches that logically relate to the
problems are rarely used,
— errors in computation or basic procedures may be
common,
— answers seem not to have been evaluated in the
context of the given problem situations.

Level 0
Portfolio is incomplete or contains no work meeting the
criteria mentioned above.

Figure 3–8 *Continued*

The rubric is written to assess students' work considering almost the same characteristics as the analytic rubric previously described. Notice that in a focused holistic rubric, each performance dimension is addressed at each level of the rubric. The rubric in Figure 3–8 is actually a five-point rubric because 0 is a possible grade for an unsatisfactory portfolio.

This rubric also specifies characteristics that distinguish the portfolio evaluated as being at the highest level. Associating the highest scores with creativity, the use of atypical approaches, the use of technology, and perseverance helps the teacher distinguish between level 4 and level 3 portfolios. The descriptors at these two levels are very much alike. Designating exemplary characteristics that go beyond the dimensions of performance defined by the rubric allows the teacher to recognize students whose portfolios demonstrate true talent. At the same time, because the students are aware of the criteria that will be used to grade their portfolios, the explicit identification of dimensions of performance gives them something to strive to attain. They may begin looking for opportunities to be creative or to show talent in working with technology.

What Happens to Portfolios After They Are Completed?

Teachers find that portfolios become treasured possessions once students have started to keep them. A portfolio should be considered to belong to the student. Sometimes teachers use a single format for a portfolio for the entire year. In such cases, the portfolio may remain in the classroom until the end of the year, because students will continue to reevaluate the pieces in their collections and perhaps replace them or add pieces. This is especially true when a portfolio is used to assess change over time. Sometimes portfolios are passed on to teachers at the next grade level. At other times, such as in state assessment models, portfolios are sent to an agency for centralized evaluation. Issues about the intended audience for the portfolio are discussed in Chapter 5.

Summary

The documentation of student learning in a portfolio can be very impressive. The challenge for the teacher is to interpret that information to serve some purpose in the educational setting. Despite the large amount of literature on educational portfolios, little direction is given to classroom teachers about how to evaluate these collections of work. Yet when the use of portfolios is challenged, the evaluation issues of reliability, validity, and objectivity are commonly raised. Chapter 5 discusses those challenges.

The central message in this chapter is that a rubric is nothing more than a written statement of what will be considered when student work is evaluated and of what standard of performance is expected. Some teachers may choose to evaluate portfolios much as they do examination papers, developing a point-allocation scale and assigning a prescribed number of points for each dimension of performance. For example, a teacher might grade a portfolio using a hundred-point scale, giving forty points for one area of performance, twenty five points each for two other areas, and ten points for organization and rationale statements in the portfolio.

This chapter describes procedures to follow to develop a more holistic and comprehensive evaluation plan. Different types of rubrics are discussed to help teachers choose the best format for evaluating their classes' portfolios. The explanations of how to identify dimensions of performance, choose a type of rubric, and select an appropriate scale outline a procedure for developing rubrics for portfolios. Those who use portfolios of different types can follow these steps to define their own rubrics. This chapter discusses the differences between rubrics for individual pieces and rubrics designed to evaluate portfolios, and the sample rubrics in this chapter demonstrate how a rubric can be used to evaluate separate pieces of work. The portfolio rubrics provide models that teachers might adapt for use in their own classrooms.

The first two chapters of this book were designed to help teachers recognize the power of the portfolio as a tool for both teaching and assessment. The discussion in this chapter is intended to help those who experiment with portfolios and prevent the day when they say, "These portfolios were great. . . . Now I have to grade the things and I'm not at all sure how to do it!"

Chapter 4

Measuring the Measurable: Creating a System of Assessment

It was conference day and Mr. Jacobs was anxious to talk to the teacher about Jane's mathematics work. He remembered his own seventh-grade experience and how his teacher had him memorize the different types of percent problems—part divided by whole, part divided by percent changed, whole divided by part—he could still remember that. It didn't seem that Jane was devoting nearly enough time to what he remembered as seventh-grade math. She even used the calculator when doing homework! He just wasn't sure that Jane was doing well—or that she was learning the kind of mathematics she would need.

Mrs. Parker smiled as she greeted Jane and her parents. The teacher began, "I'm glad you were able to come today. Jane is anxious to show you some of the things she has been doing in mathematics. Jane, would you like to begin by showing your parents the project you have started this week?"

Jane took some papers out of her folder and explained, "We had to do an opinion poll (Vance 1982), chart the results, and write a newspaper story about the results. I worked with Matt, Nate, and Caroline. We decided to ask people about their favorite meal in the cafeteria. We thought everyone was going to pick pizza, but they didn't. A lot of people liked hamburgers and french fries or chicken and mashed potatoes. That surprised us!

"We made our chart look like a menu," she continued, "and in this table we put the number of votes and the percent. You can see that forty-four students like pizza best. That was fifty-five percent. Twenty kids picked hamburgers and twelve like chicken best. Just a couple kids voted for other things they have at lunch."

Mr. Jacobs asked, "That square that is colored in, what does that show?"

Jane responded, "That is a square with one hundred little squares in it. We colored fifty-five squares red for pizza, twenty brown for hamburger, and so on. It is a picture of the percents."

The teacher said, "I'm really proud of Jane. She is such a good thinker and she does very good work when we are problem solving. Many students have a lot of difficulty with this type of work."

Mrs. Jacobs reacted, saying, "It surprises me because I was never very good at math when I was in school."

Jane's father interrupted, "That's because you didn't have a calculator. I don't like the way she depends on it. Do you really want her to use it all the time the way she does? I'm not sure she is learning the basics that she needs. Why do they have to depend on the calculator?"

"I'm glad you mentioned that, Mr. Jacobs," the teacher responded. "Jane, why don't you show your family the quiz papers in your portfolio. I use these quizzes to find out if students know the basic computational procedures and if they really understand the operations."

Jane handed two papers to her father, saying, "This is a quiz I did at the beginning of the year. And this is one we did last week. I had a lot of multiplication mistakes on the first one. Last week, we had to use multiplication and division to answer the percent questions and I did all the problems without a mistake!"

Introduction

Mr. Jacobs, like many parents, is concerned not only that his child is doing well, but also that she is being taught the things that are important. Parents' argumentative and challenging questions are frequently expressions of these two concerns. Parents who question the use of portfolios or other alternative assessment approaches probably want to hear results from traditional measures of mathematics achievement to assure them that their child is learning and doing well. The portfolio and the teacher's comments about it seem to not have the same significance to these parents as a test score would.

At the same time, the public thinks that mathematics consists of the procedures and concepts that they remember studying in school. Thus a question about new assessment approaches is often a question about the curriculum. The questions are an expression of concern that important "basic" mathematics is disappearing from the curriculum.

The teacher's conversation with Jane and her parents probably sounds familiar to every mathematics teacher who is trying to respond to the National Council of Teachers of Mathematics' curriculum and evaluation standards (1989), the professional standards for teaching (1991), and the assessment standards (1995). Such questions can only be answered by helping families understand that changes in mathematics education are comprehensive, affecting curriculum *and* instruction *and* assessment. Educators must be open and explain that new goals for students are being pursued in response to changes in society. As the *Curriculum and Evaluation Standards for School Mathematics* states, these new educational goals

> . . . reflect the importance of mathematical literacy. Toward this end, the K–12 standards articulate five general goals for all students:
>
> 1. that they learn to value mathematics,
> 2. that they become confident in their ability to do mathematics,
> 3. that they become mathematical problem solvers,
> 4. that they learn to communicate mathematically, and
> 5. that they learn to reason mathematically.
>
> These goals imply that students should be exposed to numerous and varied interrelated experiences that en-

courage them to value the mathematical enterprise, to develop mathematical habits of mind, and to understand and appreciate the role of mathematics in human affairs; that they should be encouraged to explore, to guess, and even to make and correct errors so that they gain confidence in their ability to solve complex problems; that they should read, write, and discuss mathematics; and that they should conjecture, test, and build arguments about a conjecture's validity. (1989, 5)

The NCTM statements about upgrading goals for mathematics learning propose instructional changes that will facilitate the accomplishment of the goals, and state that if curriculum is changed, the measures of learning must change as well. To support understanding about the portfolio as an assessment tool, teachers and administrators need to demystify the portfolio process, reassuring families about the progress students are making, and helping them to understand what is being taught and why it is important.

The Need for a Comprehensive Assessment System

Almost anyone who talks about assessment expresses awareness of the need for multiple approaches to assess student learning (Wiggins 1993; Swanson, Norman, and Linn 1995). Multiple choice tests are often criticized for only assessing the recall of facts or memorized information, although the truth of this criticism is often questioned (Hymes, Chafin, and Gonder 1991). Policy makers and accountability monitors make compelling arguments to continue the use of traditional standardized tests. They contend that the kind of detailed information that helps teachers make instructional decisions is not particularly efficient or effective for their purposes (Baker, Linn, and Herman 1996). Yet as long as high-stakes decisions about school effectiveness, college admissions, and placing students in special programs are based on traditional tests, those tests will have considerable influence on the assessment strategies teachers use on a daily basis. It appears clear that until the reliability and validity of each of the alternative measures is established, classroom assessment should involve a wide range of approaches so that the various purposes can be served.

Portfolio use is much less frightening when people are aware that traditional tests, quizzes, graded homework, and the like will be used as well. At the same time, actually seeing their own child's portfolio does much to help parents appreciate why a portfolio should be part of the assessment system. The following discussions will help teachers think about how to build a comprehensive system of assessment that addresses all dimensions of student learning in their classrooms. They include ideas about how to respond to the questions and concerns people might have about the use of portfolios.

Purposes of assessment

Student learning is assessed for many different reasons. Various authors elaborately discuss different uses of assessment information. Assessment results are used to inform instructional planning, to report to parents, for accountability to government or other external groups, to identify students for special programs, and the like. Just as some approaches are more effective than others to assess particular domains of knowledge, some assessment strategies are more useful than others when thinking about a particular purpose.

Portfolios serve some assessment purposes better than other strategies do, but some assessment purposes are better served by other strategies. For example, when assessment of student learning is intended to help teachers make decisions about future instruction for individual students or to communicate with parents about a child's progress, pieces included in a portfolio provide information that cannot be obtained from a coded record of work such as a test score, a teacher's grade book, or a report card. In mathematics it might be important for the teacher to notice if a student with a low score didn't finish the test, if the low score resulted from numerous random computational errors, or if the score resulted from consistent use of incorrect procedures.

On the other hand, presenting every student's portfolio to monitor the quality of curriculum or instruction in a school or district may provide more information than is needed. The time and expense of reviewing all the student work could be overwhelming and is usually avoided unless it is seen as a way to get important information that could not be gained another way. If the goal is to review programs where great variation of student performance is a matter of concern, scores on various assessments and a sample of portfolios from students whose scores fall within different ranges would provide the desired information. In other cases, district-level examination of student portfolios might not be useful. A district may, however, require that student portfolios be used in order to monitor the implementation of a new curriculum or a recommended change in emphasis.

It is important for teachers to understand the goal when portfolio use is mandated. A teacher who has a clear idea about how portfolio evaluations are to be used and who will see the portfolio will be better able to guide students in putting together portfolios that will provide useful information. For example, if a school's principal will be responsible for reviewing portfolios by having a portfolio conference with selected children, the portfolio can be merely a collection of materials with fairly simple explanations written by the children or the teacher. However, if portfolios will be collected and sent to a centralized location for review by people who have never been in the children's classroom, more elaborate explanations of the significance of pieces might be needed. This matter of who will see the portfolio is discussed in detail in Chapter 5.

Alignment of curriculum, instruction, and assessment

Almost anyone who has anything to say about assessment of student learning is apt to agree that curriculum (what students are to learn), instruction (how it will be learned), and assessment (how learning will be monitored) should be closely related. Figure 4–1 illustrates the relationships that exist when curriculum, instruction, and assessment are aligned in the way recommended by the National Council of Teachers of Mathematics (NCTM 1989). The circle is an appropriate representation of this model because the ideal is to foster a kind of seamlessness that makes it hard to distinguish an instructional task from an assessment task, and that ensures that all classroom events are consistent with the goals of

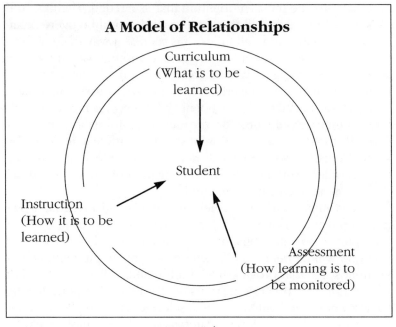

Figure 4–1

the curriculum. The student is at the center of the diagram, which connotes that all elements—curriculum, instruction, and assessment—are to be student centered.

The very fact that policymakers insist that certain types of tests be used for "accountability purposes" implies a belief that tests match the curriculum that *should* be taught. Comments from teachers that they would like to do this, or that in their classrooms but instead have to prepare students "for the test" imply that what students might learn from "this" or "that" is not tested and that the content that is to be tested must be taught instead. Among professional educators, arguments about the types of assessment that should be used are usually based on questions about what children are being taught and what they are expected to learn; about curriculum and the relationship between curriculum and assessment—questions like the ones that families have about changes in assessment in the classroom.

It is important, therefore, to think about alignment and consider the degree to which various assessment approaches match curriculum goals. The NCTM committee that wrote the 1989 standards for curriculum and evaluation described alignment in the very first statement about evaluation:

Methods and tasks for assessing students' learning should be aligned with the curriculum's—

- goals, objectives, and mathematical content;
- relative emphasis given to various topics and processes and their relationships;
- instructional approaches and activities, including the use of calculators, computers, and manipulatives. (p. 193)

This description provides a basis for thinking about the relative merits of various assessment approaches.

Matching the curriculum   All mathematics assessment instruments or strategies claim to match with the goals and objectives of the curriculum. Curriculum-embedded tests, such as the end-of-chapter tests in textbooks, frequently identify the pages where content related to a test item can be found. Standardized test companies publish lists of the content assessed by their instruments, and often even develop guides that show the match between their tests and state curriculum frameworks or guides and commonly used textbooks.

Yet a report of the National Commission on Testing and Public Policy (1990) raises questions about the completeness of the match. The commission called for greater public accountability regarding what is tested and the results that are reported. Its report said that "tests need to be more accurately labeled, results more constructively reported, and evidence as to what tests do and do not measure made more accessible" (p. 32). The dilemma seems to be that test designers are going to great lengths to describe what is tested, yet little information is given about what is *not* tested or about what the results mean and how they should be interpreted in light of the total school curriculum.

85

Matching the topic emphasis prescribed by the curriculum   Examining the match between the curriculum and the assessment's emphasis on content reveals the shortcomings of certain tests. For example, school curriculum guides usually assert that an important goal is for students to learn to apply mathematics in everyday life and to support the development of real understanding of the concepts and ideas that are studied. Yet the tests we use do not emphasize content that would help students achieve that goal.

Part of the problem is time. Teacher-made tests or those printed in textbooks are typically planned to be administered within a specific period of time, perhaps a forty-minute class period. Standardized tests, too, are typically administered in a set time period. As a result, items on the tests are designed to suit the allocated time. When the examination must be completed within a limited time, tests cannot include problems that require a great deal of time to complete, or problems whose solution strategy is not fairly obvious. If some students choose a less-efficient method than others, or spend too much time thinking about a single item, they might be penalized because they will not complete all of the items on the test. Their final score would not be an appropriate index of what they know.

Given these constraints, most items on tests end up looking a great deal like most of the exercises in textbooks dealing with straightforward computational or algorithmic procedures. Few, if any, items require students to solve applied problems or relate deeper understanding of the concepts studied. Yet judgments about student learning are based on the students' performance on such tests, which have often emphasized the most simplistic dimensions of the curriculum. The community member who complains about the delivery boy or the clerk who cannot count change may well be talking about a student who makes good grades on tests that emphasize textbook content and assess applied knowledge in only a cursory fashion.

Matching instructional approaches and activities   The importance of the recommendation that assessment should be aligned with the instructional approaches and activities used in a classroom may be puzzling. Part of the reason for this recommendation is that it is difficult to separate the content of instruction from the pedagogical method. For example, if students are using a calculator in class, they are both learning about the mathematics that is being used and developing skill with the calculator. When students use a model, such as pattern blocks, to communicate ideas about fractions, they are developing both an understanding of fractions and the ability to model mathematical ideas with concrete objects.

Ideally, students should learn to communicate using both models and symbols. They should also learn the mathematics topics in the curriculum and be expected to use calculators and other tools of mathematics. A good assessment system will allow students to use alternative strategies to communicate their understanding and will assess whether they can use symbols, models, and other tools effectively in their mathematical work. The point is that the use of different instructional strategies frequently results in expanding, or limiting, the learner's mathematical experience. Incorporating questions that parallel the broad range of instructional activities provides a detailed picture of what students know and are able to do.

Traditional tests, be they commercially produced or teacher-made, be they standardized or not, have limited ability to match curriculum and instruction. That does not mean that such tests do not provide important information about some areas of student learning. What it does mean is that the use of other approaches to assessment in conjunction with traditional testing (at levels where it is developmentally appropriate) is likely to support the true alignment of curriculum, instruction, and assessment, and result in more-accurate assessment of student learning.

The place of the portfolio in an assessment system

Chapter 1 describes the portfolios that serve as an organizational structure for saving and reporting the overall picture of a learner's work. When this is the case, the portfolio *becomes* the assessment system and all other assessment information is included in the portfolio collection. However, other types of portfolios described in Chapter 1 tell the story of only one or two dimensions of a student's development. Because the design of a quality assessment system requires that attention be given to *all* dimensions of learning, it is important to coordinate the focus of the portfolio and of other assessment strategies.

Integrating the portfolio into a plan for using multiple assessments
One approach to constructing an assessment system is to begin by identifying the range of knowledge and ability that should be assessed. Curriculum frameworks and curriculum guides would be likely places to begin. However, in some cases curriculum guides are mere outlines of topics in mathematics content that ignore other important areas of learning, such as communication. In other cases, curriculum documents have been updated to include the newly defined areas of mathematics learning; such guides would be a helpful starting place.

A recent publication by the Mathematical Sciences Education Board (MSEB 1993) identifies areas that served as the focus for the board's development of prototypical assessment tasks for fourth grade. This project was in response to a challenge to mathematics educators to show what is meant by ". . . mathematical power and what new and more demanding standards will mean for our young people." The areas of focus for assessment proposed by the MSEB, especially the following five, will be useful in planning a classroom assessment system.

- *Mathematical Content*: Assessment should ". . . reflect the 'spirit' of the reform movement. . . . tasks should incorporate a variety of mathematics, particularly in areas such as statistics, geometry, and probability that are least often emphasized in traditional K–4 programs."
- *Mathematical connections*: Students must connect what they learn to the areas of mathematics, to other school subjects, and to life outside the classroom.
- *Thoughtful approaches*: Assessment should involve higher-order thinking and cognitive complexity.
- *Mathematical communication:* The assessment ". . . should emphasize the importance of communicating results—not just isolated answers but mathematical representations and chains of reasoning. . . .Children should have opportunities to explain their thinking to others, and to write explanations of their approaches."

- *Rich opportunities* "The tasks should let children solve problems via a variety of creative strategies; demonstrate talents (artistic, spatial, verbal); invent mathematics that (to them) is new; recognize opportunities to use and apply mathematics; and show what they can do (as opposed to what they cannot do)."

The categories formulated by MSEB can be used in conjunction with local curriculum guides to develop a framework for the assessment system. Although the MSEB targeted fourth grade, the categories can be adapted and expanded to suit other grade levels.

The following conversation among a group of third-grade teachers illustrates a strategy for developing an assessment plan using the MSEB list as a starting place.

Barbara entered the room and greeted everyone, saying, "I'm glad we're going to have this meeting. I have been doing all these new things in assessment but I just can't get a handle on how it all fits together."

"Let's get started," Phyllis suggested. "I have the feeling we have a big job ahead of us. Mr. Barnes gave us this outline and asked us to try to expand it for our grade level and list what assessments we are using for each area of learning."

"Let's start with the math content section," said Tom. "We could use the sections of our curriculum guide: Numbers and Numeration, Operations, Geometry, Measurement, Patterns and Relationships, Fractions, and so on."

Barbara commented, "That's a good place to begin, but what about this stuff about statistics and probability? Do we really have to put this in for third grade? Our curriculum guide doesn't say much about that."

Tanya answered, "You do a lot of that in your class. Every time I come in your room your kids are graphing something. And you do all those prediction activities after doing the observation lessons in science. That would be a good way to think about this connections category, too."

"But wait a minute!" said Phyllis, "How do we bring this information around to thinking about the assessment plan? I'm not sure what we are doing. Doesn't Barnes want an assessment plan?"

Barbara responded, "You're right, but I think we are on the right track. In this section on content, for some things my quizzes and assignments are what I look at to see if the kids are catching on, but something like probability and statistics, I never really thought of testing on that! I'm not sure I could write questions that would get at what I want to know about the kids' understanding. I just look at their projects and papers and listen to the answers they give during class and I get a sense of when they understand."

Tom commented, "That would be a good topic for the portfolio at our grade level. We aren't supposed to teach all the vocabulary they do in upper grades. We just want kids to understand how to use and make sense of data. When I look at papers from the past month—it's the writing, the explanations, the improvement in their graphs—that I notice. I don't know how I could make a test that would show that."

Phyllis responded, "That's a good idea. What if we plan to assess communication, statistics, and probability with the portfolio? As we move on we'll see if there is anything else we should put in the portfolio."

"This isn't so hard," said Barbara. "Let's see if any other math content should be put in the portfolio. What about measurement? That's a big thing for our students to learn."

Tom responded, "I kind of like the projects we do during the Measurement Festival. If we graded those, and gave a quiz on the units of measurement, we would have a pretty good idea what the students know. I don't want that portfolio to get too big."

Tanya said, "That's a good idea. We'll assess measurement using projects and quizzes. Are there any other topics we can talk about?"

Clearly, if important kinds of learning are not adequately assessed by classroom tests, those areas are a likely focus for a portfolio. A plan of the assessment strategies the teachers decided to use is shown in Figure 4–2. In the planning conversation they were able to identify particular areas where the portfolio would complement the other assessment approaches used in mathematics. Typically, teachers will want to have some experience with the portfolio before trying to map out a complete plan like the one in Figure 4–2.

The plan shown in Figure 4–2 demonstrates the integration of various assessment strategies into a system, and the combination creates an appropriate awareness of what students know and are able to do. In situations where the results of all assessments must be combined to determine a final grade for the report period or the semester, one further question must be pursued: how can the various assessments be combined to ensure that assessments of the important areas of the curriculum appropriately influence the final grade?

One strategy would be to consider the five dimensions being assessed and make judgments about the relative importance of each. For example, teachers might feel that the math content area is the most important, and that at least 50 percent of the grade should be determined by that area, while mathematical communication, mathematical connections, and thoughtful approaches are about equally important. Based on that decision, a combined grade could be calculated for communication, connections, and approaches, and a separate grade would be determined for math content. The combination of the math content grade with the single grade for the other three areas would result in the desired emphasis on content.

A problem does emerge when teachers use a point-count or percent system and the numerical scores for categories do not represent the categories' significance in the final decision about how much has been learned. For example, if each area was represented by assignments, tests, and such and was scored and averaged using percents, the highest possible score would be 100. At the same time, if a five-point holistic rubric was used for the portfolio, that five-point score would have little significance when combined with all other scores.

To counteract this, it would be important to convert the rubric score for each student by multiplying by twenty. Thus, a score of 5 from the rubric would count as 100 in the final calculation of a grade, a score of 4 would be 80, and so on. When an

Third-Grade Assessment Plan

	First Quarter	Second Quarter	Third Quarter	Fourth Quarter
Math Content				
—Numbers & Numeration	T & A	T	T & A & I	T & I
—Operations	T & A	T & A	T & A	T & A
—Geometry	T & P	T & P	A & P	I & A
—Measurement	T & I	T & P	T & P	A & P
—Patterns & Relationships	A & P	A & P	A & P	A & P
—Fractions	T & A	T & A	T & A	T & A
—Probability	P	P	P	P
—Statistics	P	P	P	P
—Problem Solving	A & P	I & P	T & P	I & P
Mathematical Connections				
—within math	P	P	P	P
—to other subjects	P	P	P	P
—to life outside classroom	P	P	P	P

Thoughtful Approaches		
—Using models	P	P
—higher-order thinking	P	P
—finish complex tasks	P	P
—find alternative approaches	P	P
Mathematical Communication		
—uses terms	P & I	P & I
—makes graphs, tables, drawings	P & I	P & I
—gives examples	P & I	P & I
—provides details	P & I	P & I

Key: P=portfolio T=tests and quizzes A=assignments I=investigations or projects

Figure 4–2

analytic rubric is used the conversion is a little different. If an analytic rubric involves four dimensions, each graded on a five-point scale, a student's scores from each dimension would be totaled (the highest score would be 20) and that total would be multiplied by five (the highest score would be 100).

In short, the assessment system must not only be designed to assess all areas of importance, it must also be designed to control how performance in each of the areas of learning affects the scoring scheme. If this is not monitored carefully, the least important aspects of performance may outweigh the other areas because there are more scores in the wrong area. This dilemma is the same as the dilemma of tests not matching the *emphasis* in the curriculum. Some tests have many more items that assess computational skills than problem solving and conceptual understanding. The total score, therefore, is influenced to a greater extent by the computational skills questions because of the large number of items in that area. Some tests attempt to counteract this using a variety of strategies; however, the domain of knowledge covered by the problem-solving and conceptual parts of tests is so large that the emphasis on performance on computation still exists.

A portfolio equivalent to a chapter test   In some cases where the classroom assessment system is rather simple, it is helpful to tell students that the portfolio grade will be equivalent to a test grade. This is especially useful if the portfolio focuses on something that is not evaluated in other ways. For example, certain cross-discipline or interdisciplinary abilities are important for students to develop whether or not they are in schools where teachers use an interdisciplinary approach. The NCTM standards (1989) identify assessing the development of students' awareness of connections between mathematics and other subjects as a central goal, yet teachers rarely incorporate such assessment into their classroom systems. Most teachers agree that it is important for students to learn research and inquiry skills, but assessment of these skills happens rather haphazardly in most settings.

The portfolio can be a useful tool for evaluating the awareness of connections. Teachers may wish to have the grade on a *connections portfolio* count as much as a test score when final grades are determined. Figure 4–3 shows an outline that teachers

Portfolio Outline
Inquiry and Research Knowledge and Ability

Student Name _____

GENERAL INQUIRY STRATEGIES   Assignment I. D.*
(a) doing experiments or simulations   _____   _____
(b) using library or reference skills   _____   _____
(c) reading reports, accounts, etc.   _____   _____
(d) data collection and management   _____   _____
(e) use of technology   _____   _____

MATHEMATICS
(f) make graphs, tables, charts   _____   _____
(g) explain information contained on
     graphs, tables, charts   _____   _____
(h) make inferences or predictions based
     on numerical data   _____   _____
(i) evaluate conclusions, inferences, or
     predictions   _____   _____

LANGUAGE ARTS
(j) write accurate and interesting reports   _____   _____
(k) consult literature from several genres   _____   _____

SCIENCE
(l) design and carry out investigations   _____   _____
(m) make and justify predictions   _____   _____

SOCIAL STUDIES
(n) identify critical variables in the social
     context   _____   _____
(o) make and justify inferences   _____   _____

THE ARTS
(p) use media creatively in portraying
     findings   _____   _____
(q) identify critical attributes to be
     considered in research   _____   _____

*Select two pieces of work for each category. If one piece fits several categories just indicate by title or date that you are using that piece to demonstrate learning in several areas.

Figure 4–3

might find useful for assessing connections through consideration of students' research and inquiry skills in different school subjects. This type of portfolio might be useful in a departmentalized or team-teaching arrangement, where students have different teachers for different subjects. A team of teachers could determine particular areas of student development to work on in each class. The outline would also be useful if a teacher or team were using an interdisciplinary or thematic approach to lessons in different disciplines, and inquiry or research skills were being emphasized in the unit.

The first section of the outline relates to general skills that a student might acquire in several subjects. Other sections relate to the research and inquiry abilities that would be the focus of activities and experiences in particular subject areas. The same abilities might also be employed in other areas, but the goal in this case is to monitor the connections made between research and inquiry done in different subjects. For this type of portfolio, students are directed to select two or three pieces to show their accomplishment in each category. They might also be challenged to find pieces of work from different subjects to document their learning. For example, students might select a report written in social studies class to demonstrate their ability to explain information using graphs, a category under mathematics.

If a connections portfolio is graded using a rubric, the strategies described previously to equate rubric scores to other assessments would be useful. Some teachers prefer to evaluate connections portfolios in much the same way they would grade a test, giving a certain number of points for each category. For example, each of the seventeen items in the outline could be given a point value of five, for a total of eighty-five. Fifteen points could be allocated for organization, table of contents, rationale statements, evidence of reflection, and other overall matters the teacher wishes to consider. This "grading rule" approach is sometimes easier to use at first; teachers might later be able to develop a rubric that will work as well.

An Example of a System

The *Work Sampling System* (WSS), developed over a period of years and field tested in sites around the country (Meisels et al.

1994), exemplifies the potential of an approach that uses a variety of assessment strategies to monitor many different areas of learning. The system is designed for use in preschool through grade five and documents a child's progress in seven different areas: personal and social development, language and literacy, mathematical thinking, scientific thinking, social studies, the arts, and physical development. The assessment of mathematical thinking targets six areas of learning: approach to mathematical thinking, patterns and relationships, number concepts and operations, geometry and spatial relations, measurement, and probability and statistics. Each of these areas is fully described and characterized in the WSS materials to help teachers determine what student performances and products can be used as the basis for assessment decisions.

In using WSS, teachers keep anecdotal records of both formal and informal observations, use checklists to record judgments about student performance, and work with students to keep portfolios that show growth over time. Three times each year (fall, winter, and spring), the portfolio collection is defined and the teacher completes the checklist and writes a narrative summary report about each student. In many schools the summary report and the portfolio are shared with parents, taking the place of traditional report cards.

The design of the Work Sampling System portfolio requires that a teacher focus selection of some pieces of children's work on core areas that are the same for all students in the classroom. These common core items facilitate judgment about how well a child is doing compared to peers. Other pieces of a child's portfolio are selected to highlight the unique characteristics of each child's learning. For one child, a piece might show how well explanations of problem-solving procedures are written; for another, an item might illustrate the development of spatial skills. In fall, winter, and spring, the collection is closed and a new one is started. At the end of the year, the three collections portray the development of each child's mathematical thinking in the areas that were the focus of the collection.

The WSS checklists and the guidelines that define their use are an important part of the system. The checklists are based on national standards of performance and knowledge of child development. Teachers can use the checklists to compare a child's performance to national standards by carefully evaluating the child's work in light of the objectives outlined in the checklists and guidelines.

Each of the elements of the Work Sampling System serves a function in the assessment process. Learners' progress is monitored carefully. The information teachers gather in anecdotal records and during the periodic reviews of checklists and portfolios provides a true picture of what each learner knows and is able to do in a variety of situations and circumstances.

Any classroom assessment system should have components that serve the function of the components of WSS. The system should assess students' progress in light of national standards, allow comparison of students within a classroom, and identify the unique strengths and talents of individuals. The first two functions are in part addressed by standardized tests. However, such tests only offer comparisons for limited areas of learning. A comprehensive system must strive for more than that limited basis of comparison. Thus the use of performance assessment (Shannon and Zawojewki 1995) and portfolios become a vital part of any comprehensive assessment system.

Summary

A quality assessment program possesses a number of different characteristics. The first thing to be considered is alignment. Does the assessment system match the curriculum and instructional methods used? The search for alignment relates to whether or not student learning is assessed in light of *all* the goals of curriculum. The assessment must also weight areas of learning in a way that matches the intended goals for learning. At the same time the traditional question of validity, reliability, and fairness must also be considered.

Based on the premise that different assessment strategies are better than others to monitor particular areas of student learning, one of the challenges to developing a system is to include a number of different assessment sources to provide the best possible information about students' learning in all relevant areas. At the same time, the variety of purposes for assessment must be considered. Different individuals and agencies will want assessment information to address different questions. It is important that accurate information about students that can be used to inform judgments and decisions be made available.

Finally, the decision to use portfolios for assessment purposes relates to and affects many aspects of classroom life. Teachers and students assume different roles, as described in Chapter 2, so the kinds of activities that serve as the basis for evaluations change. Teachers must include in the assessment plan a wide range of tasks that will challenge students while providing them with opportunities to use their knowledge in applied contexts. All of this requires considerable effort and commitment to the idea that educators must find ways to assess all dimensions of learning instead of accepting traditional explanations of what can be measured and how assessment should be done.

Chapter 5

Conversations and Questions: Do I Really Want to Use Portfolios?

Milford School District had decided to encourage teachers to implement portfolio assessment in the middle schools. The teachers had just finished a two-day staff development program on portfolio use. Emotions ran high in the faculty room as teachers arrived for school. Andrew commented, "The thing I liked best was the speaker's definition of portfolios, 'Portfolios are something that are mandated by someone who has never kept one.' That says it all for me! I've been teaching for fifteen years and I have seen such fads come and go. This is one time I'd like to sit this one out."

Pat responded, "Good grief, that speaker had so many good ideas—and what she said makes so much sense. I can't believe that you are ready to call it a fad— before we even talk about what we might do."

Marlene looked up from her papers and reported, "You know, they have been using them at Wallace Creek School for a couple of years. My neighbor teaches there and she seems to like portfolios. She told me it is hard at first, but each year it takes a little less work."

"Yeah," Andrew said, "that's what they always say. It will get easier . . . the kids will catch on . . . other teachers really like it." The bell rang and he walked toward the door saying, "My students are doing just fine. They do pretty well when they get to high school, too. Keeping a math scrap book isn't going to help them get to college!"

Introduction

Expectations, beliefs, and myths about portfolios vary significantly. Unfortunately, those who have no experience with the assessment strategy are often the most impassioned opponents or the most enthusiastic advocates when portfolios are discussed. The preceding chapters provide explanations, examples, and suggestions that are meant to be helpful to those who are beginning to use portfolios. This chapter talks about the issues and questions that arise when portfolio assessment is implemented in various contexts. It also presents information to help teachers understand rationales and goals for portfolio use.

High-Stakes Assessment

Professionals are increasingly relying on portfolios to support important decisions about students and school programs. Assessment that is used for accountability purposes; for program evaluation; or to inform decisions about student placement, promotion, or retention is referred to as *high-stakes assessment.* A number of states, including Kentucky and Vermont, have integrated a portfolio component into their state-level mathematics assessment systems. Much of what has already been suggested about using portfolios is exemplified in such large-scale uses of portfolios. In each case, the portfolio collection is focused to assess only certain dimensions of student learning, and the portfolio is used in combination with other assessment approaches. Those who wish to implement portfolios have much to learn from the portfolio experiences in state assessment programs.

The Vermont mathematics portfolio, for example, is used for assessment at grades four, eight, and ten in combination with a criterion referenced test (CRT) and a performance assessment. A report by the National Education Goals Panel (1996) characterizes the purpose of the various components of the Vermont system. The report says the portfolio is intended to "Support instructional improvement and monitor student performance against benchmarks," and that the CRT and the performance assessment are used to "monitor portfolio scoring and provide school level comparative data."

Expectation: The portfolio as a tool to enhance instruction
The description of the purpose of the components of the Vermont mathematics assessment introduces several issues related to portfolio use. First, no other form of high-stakes assessment has ever been associated with the expectation that the assessment will enhance *instruction*, as is the case with portfolios. Statewide assessment programs are typically valued because they hold schools and teachers accountable for *what* is taught. There has never been an expectation that another assessment approach would influence instruction, that is, *how* content is taught.

The idea that portfolio use will lead to enhanced instruction appears frequently in the literature and in professional conversations. The NCTM Assessment Standards for Mathematics (1995) suggest that a major accomplishment of the shift to alternative assessments is the degree to which the new approaches lead to enhanced instruction. This position is a logical one. The earlier chapters of this book suggest that effective use of portfolios provides insight into broader dimensions of student learning. If, indeed, alternative assessment approaches provide better information than traditional strategies, the teacher will have a better basis for making decisions about student needs. Thus there is an expectation that instruction will be more tailored to support student learning.

Traditional assessment that leads only to consideration of straightforward right or wrong answers does not help teachers recognize patterns of difficulty, the use of faulty algorithms, or misconceptions that inhibit success in learning different mathematics topics. The scores in a grade book only reveal the consistency of success or failure; they do not provide details that allow teachers to notice the relationships or patterns of student difficulty across time. Teachers who know more about why students are being successful or not will be able to prepare instruction that is focused on helping students succeed where they had difficulty in the past. A portfolio has the power to enhance instruction if it really provides such information. At this time, however, little research has been done to validate the legitimacy of this expectation.

Portfolio use might also lead to enhanced instruction when

teachers review portfolios to evaluate their own teaching and review the instructional approaches they are using. If the work in the portfolio does not provide evidence of creativity or ingenuity, and does not lead to insight about students' ability to use higher-order thinking, teachers might begin to think critically about their teaching approaches, and to look for tasks, activities, and experiences that would result in student products that provide information that could serve as the basis of assessment for *all* areas of student learning. In some cases, teachers might realize that students are not pursuing goals related to some areas of learning within the instruction being offered, and that they need to diversify the opportunities offered to students.

Portfolios can also serve as a supervisory tool for those who work with teachers. In fact, a review of student portfolios by those outside the classroom provides information that can be used to evaluate both a program and teaching. It is possible to monitor the effectiveness of a program by looking at the samples of student work in a portfolio. The review will reveal whether students are having special difficulty with particular elements of the program, and if the program supports learning of especially challenging areas of the curriculum.

Student portfolios also are useful to support teacher development. If a new program is being implemented, the degree to which the program is being used successfully in different classrooms can be examined by considering the kinds of tasks and activities that are documented in student portfolios. If a portfolio doesn't contain any student work that is related to the goals and form of a new program, the teacher may not be implementing the new program completely. At the same time, student work on elements of a new program will reveal which teachers are having success with the implementation. Staff development efforts could then target the aspects of the program that are posing difficulty for teachers.

Some schools ask teachers to prepare a professional portfolio as part of their teacher evaluation process. The inclusion of student work in such collections offers powerful evidence of a teacher's success in the classroom. Teachers who have students' portfolios will have strong evidence to include in their own professional portfolios.

Expectation: Reliability and validity

Consideration of the National Education Goals Panel report (1996), leads to another issue related to portfolio assessment. The report explains that Vermont's criterion referenced test and performance assessment are used to "monitor portfolio scoring and provide school level comparative data." The reliability and validity of portfolio assessment are frequently challenged (Elbow 1994). It is no surprise that a high-stakes assessment, such as a state-mandated one, would need some check on evaluations based on portfolios.

Although state-level assessments that use portfolios standardize the evaluation of student work in every way possible, questions about subjectivity, inconsistency, and inaccuracy are still raised. Further, many people question how ten or fewer pieces of student work can possibly provide sufficient information to make conclusions about student learning. If school-level comparisons are to be made across a state, there is a true need to monitor the reliability of portfolio scoring and to review the correlation of portfolio scores with scores from more traditional measures. This has been done in most of the early state assessment programs that incorporate portfolio use (Klein et al. 1995).

When a portfolio is planned and implemented within a single classroom, the issues of reliability and validity are not so complex. If the teacher uses a consistent set of standards to evaluate the students' work, and if those standards are made public in a rubric or written grading guidelines, the issue of subjectivity is no different than for other types of assessment. The possibility of teacher bias remains the same as it would be for many other types of teacher-graded assignments. If the focus of the portfolio is clear and it is coordinated with other assessment strategies used in the classroom, a complete and comprehensive report of student learning is accomplished.

A greater challenge exists when several teachers at a grade level, all the teachers in a school, or all the teachers in a school district implement a system of portfolio assessment. In such cases, it is essential that teachers discuss the focus of the portfolio and how it will be evaluated. Agreement must be reached about how the portfolios will be graded, and the consistency of evaluation from teacher to teacher and school to school must be monitored.

A portfolio assessment plan is flawed if the same portfolio would receive different grades when evaluated by different teachers.

This issue, however, should not prevent teachers or schools from attempting to use portfolios. When teacher-made tests are the basis of evaluation and some teachers are known to make easier or harder tests than others, it doesn't cause everyone to lose faith in the test as an instrument of evaluation. Rather, if inconsistency in testing is a problem, teachers or administrators work to design more consistent tests. They may even develop grade-level or district-wide tests to monitor learning from classroom to classroom and establish guidelines for grading students. Similarly, cooperating in the development of rubrics and holding training or practice sessions on their use can lead to school- or district-wide consistency in portfolio evaluation.

If portfolios are to be used to compare students within a school or across a district, some system of validating the consistency of grading can be employed. For example, a random sample of portfolios from each school or classroom could be gathered and evaluated by a single panel of teachers. When the relationship between portfolio grades and grades from other assessments vary dramatically, there may be a need to look more closely to ensure the adequacy of the rubric and consistency in its use.

Forming New Partnerships

Mr. Perez, the district curriculum coordinator, initiated the last discussion of the day, saying, "I am so glad so many of you were willing to come to this meeting to share examples of how you have been using portfolios in your classrooms. I was especially glad to see that we have teachers from many different grade levels and from almost every building in the district. Today, you have had opportunities to look at student portfolios from one another's classrooms and to talk about them in small groups. I asked you to keep a record of things your group noticed and things you wondered about as you examined and discussed portfolios from other teachers' classrooms. Would one of the groups like to volunteer to be first? Okay, Robert?"

"Most of those in our group teach English or humanities in the middle school. We noticed how much teachers in elementary schools are using writing across the curriculum. I couldn't believe how well those second graders could write about mathematics. But sometimes we weren't sure what the pieces of work meant. We couldn't really tell why some pieces were in the collection."

Marcia, from another group, continued, "Yes, we had the same problem, and sometimes wondered what we could evaluate by looking at the portfolio. We noticed that it was easier to understand portfolios where students had written statements about the collection or about the pieces. . . ."

The discussion of the portfolio process in Chapter 2 describes the partnership that is established between teachers and learners as students become more involved in reflection, assessment, and goal setting. The idea of new partnerships with families is also suggested. Depending on the type of portfolio and how it is used, other partnerships evolve among the members of the professional community within the school or district. The conversation from a school district staff meeting that introduced this section demonstrates that it is important to think about these partnerships from the very beginning when planning portfolio use.

Who will see the portfolio?

One of the things teachers noticed at the district meeting was that some portfolios were hard to understand. This is a common dilemma when portfolios are not assembled with thought about future audiences. Probably every child from that classroom could have talked about the collection and helped others understand its purpose and the reason particular pieces were included. However, when a portfolio is going to be shared with "outsiders," some strategy must be employed to translate the meaning of the collection for them.

Previous chapters talk about strategies that not only support student reflection, but also make collections meaningful to those outside the classroom who might see them. Such strategies include introductory letters from children, tables of contents, check-

106

lists, and portfolio outlines. Mrs. Avery's story in the introduction to Chapter 1 tells how she introduced portfolio use in first grade. Her students' collections alone would not have been meaningful to an outsider, but because she selected the pieces that would be included and had every child save the same pieces, Mrs. Avery could have written a common letter from the teacher explaining what was included in the collection and why.

Figure 2–5 shows a format suggested for use when portfolios are to be shared at school-family conferences. Both the teacher and the student complete a statement about the collection; these comments are presented when family members first see the portfolio. A teacher's statement on a child's portfolio could help families notice important things about the collection. Figure 5–1 shows what a parent might see as an introduction to a portfolio.

The teacher's and student's statements direct the family member's attention to important aspects of the collection. Inviting the family member to record reactions or thoughts strengthens the partnership between school and family by involving the parent in the evaluation of the child's learning in a meaningful way. Monitoring the student's progress becomes a cooperative effort that involves the family, teacher, and student. A school-family conference that concentrates on pieces of a student's work, rather than the entries in a grade book, provides better information to the family and invites meaningful discussion about strategies that might support the student's learning in school and at home.

Another strategy suggested in Chapter 2 communicates information about the collection to anyone who might see the portfolio. Having students write statements about what they learned on each piece as they add it to the collection also helps them remember the significance of pieces done weeks before. This strategy might be especially helpful when students will be asked to share their collections with other teachers or the principal. A principal who is invited to come to the class and listen to small groups of children as they explain their portfolios will gain insight into what a teacher is trying to accomplish and the progress that students are making. A teacher who is frustrated by the pressure to use standardized test scores may invite administrators to portfolio review sessions to demonstrate what is being accomplished and the effort that students are putting into their work.

Conference Sheet

The pieces of work in this portfolio were done during this report period. Students selected pieces for this portfolio to show what they are learning in mathematics, and how well they are doing. The teacher and student wrote their thoughts about the portfolio. We'd like you to do the same. Look over the portfolio and what the teacher and student wrote on this sheet. Then write your thoughts about the work you see or about anything else you want to discuss in the conference.

Student Name ___ Bridget _____ Date _____

Student's Comments	Teacher's Comments	Family's Comments
I corrected all mistakes on my papers. I know how to do these now. My graphs and diagrams are really good. My goal is to read story problems two times before I start to do them.	These pieces of work show some of the things Bridget has been doing. Her work is what I expect of a fourth-grade student. I agree with Bridget's goal that she should try to read problems more carefully so that she does not miss important information.	

Figure 5–1

108

The overall appearance of the portfolio also becomes a matter of concern when it is to be shared outside the classroom. Chapter 1 recommends that teachers remember that the portfolio process is much more important than the final product. Folded construction paper or file folders are typically sufficient for a classroom portfolio or a working portfolio. When the collection is going to be shown or sent to others, teachers usually want to pay more attention to the final product. Teachers might want students to use fresh folders when the collection is finalized. If the portfolio is cumulative across the year, pocket folders might be used to show earlier work on one side and new additions on the other. There are probably as many ideas for containers as there are teachers. Two things should be kept in mind when selecting a format for final packaging. First, can these containers be stored conveniently if they are to be kept in the classroom? Second, since the contents are the most important thing, does the container distract attention from the contents?

Demystifying the portfolio process

The introduction to this chapter suggests that the most impassioned opponents of portfolio use frequently know very little about it. Unfortunately, alternative assessment approaches have been inappropriately connected to controversial movements such as "outcomes-based education" (Baron and Boschee 1996). Successful implementation of the portfolio process requires that teachers take responsibility for providing information to families and others who are in a position to influence school practice. Those who are uninformed cannot support the effort and often become opponents because of their lack of understanding.

> Mrs. Phillips greeted the parents and families as they entered her room for the classroom meeting part of the first open house of the year. After responding to questions about the principal's remarks about the new reading program that would be used at the school this year, she began, "We also will be changing some of the things we do in the fifth grade. We have always had students keep folders of work to share with you at certain times. This year we are going to be more systematic with the mathematics

folders because we want you to have a better opportunity to see more about what your children are learning in school and how they are doing.

"We are going to call the folders 'assessment portfolios.' Each report period, the fifth-grade teachers will give students an outline of what they are to include in the collection of work during that period. The outline will also tell what teachers will consider when grading the portfolios. Whenever students finish an assignment, report, or project, they will decide if they want to save that piece of work for the final collection. If they do, they will put it in their working portfolio and they will attach a note telling what they learned while doing the work and why they think they should save it.

"At the end of the report period, I will help them decide which pieces they want to include in the final assessment portfolio. You'll be able to see the first portfolio when you come to the first school-family conference day. Mrs. Ross, do you want to say something?"

Mrs. Ross began, "I read something about these portfolios. It said that portfolios let kids off the hook and they don't work as hard in school. Aren't you worried about that?"

"That is a good question, Mrs. Ross," Mrs. Phillips responded. "How many of you are concerned about that?"

A number of people raised their hands. Mrs. Phillips explained, "A lot of teachers had the same concern when we started to plan portfolios. We decided that we will continue to give tests, quizzes, and assignments as we always have so that we can be sure the students are doing what they always did and hopefully a little more. We think the portfolios will challenge students and motivate them to try new things. . . ."

Mrs. Phillips' conversation was planned to help families understand what the class was going to do with the new kind of mathematics folder. She explained how the assessment portfolios would be alike and differ from the folders of work students usually took home to their families. She probably told the parents that the portfolios would be graded, and talked about how the collections would influence report cards. She would have also explained special policies about editing work or limiting the number of pieces.

Perhaps the most important information to provide in such an explanation is why teachers have decided to use portfolios. Some of the points teachers may wish to make to families are

1. The portfolio will help everyone see how much progress students are making during the year.
2. Everyone who sees the portfolio will know the kind of things the students are studying and how well they are doing.
3. Seeing students' work tells you more about what they know and are able to do than scores in a grade book or grades on a report card do.
4. Seeing samples of student work can help you talk with your children about the goals they might pursue during the next report period.
5. If you are not sure how well a student is doing compared to other students of the same age, you can ask the teacher.
6. A portfolio of work that is passed on to next year's teacher is much better than a mere grade in helping the teacher plan instruction that builds on students' strengths and addresses areas of weakness.

Whether talking to professional educators or to members of families and the community, the most important thing to do is to introduce the idea of portfolios in terms of familiar practices. Among professionals, only the greatest risk-takers and the most confident will be willing to give portfolios a try, if they are introduced as something brand new and revolutionary. Family groups are apt to be more skeptical than enthusiastic if the assessment portfolio is introduced as a strange and mysterious key to better assessment of learning. In truth, the portfolio is neither magical nor mysterious. It is merely an expansion and revision of things that many teachers have routinely done in classrooms for years.

New Visions of Teaching, Learning, and Assessment

The current effort to reform assessment is a matter of concern to virtually every stakeholder in education. Much of the development of alternative assessment practices has occurred through collaborations between those who have traditionally been "curriculum and instruction" experts and those who are "measurement" experts. The results have led to progress in education for the most part. This book explores portfolio use primarily from the perspective of classroom teachers. It is also important to discuss issues in the field of educational measurement that have supported the recent changes in assessment practice.

A number of authors have explored the assessment reform movement from historical and philosophical perspectives (Glaser and Silver 1994; Garcia and Pearson 1994; Wolf et al. 1991). Such research commonly addresses the changes that have occurred in society. Society seems to be committed to assessment methods that were designed decades ago to rank or sort people. Test results were primarily normative and communicated comparisons of individuals. In fact, such tests were, and still are, developed to include items that will ensure that not everyone gets everything right. They include items that some will miss so that students can be ranked.

This made sense in a school setting that grouped students homogenously, that wanted to define ability groups or tracks. Many have experienced school settings where the college-bound and the trade-bound students could be identified by eighth grade, if not earlier. But changes in society make this a flawed system. There are fewer jobs for students who fall in the lower ends of the ranking, because of automation and modern technology. If schools are to continue to be responsive to the needs of society, they must realize that even the best assessment systems from the mid-twentieth century will not serve society well in the twenty-first century.

Emerging views about teaching and learning also lead to questions about traditional assessment methods. Shared responsibility between teacher and learner is proposed in the Chapter 2 description of the process of portfolio use. This view is that of a "constructivist" (DeVries and Kohlberg 1987) and fosters a true interest in how students think and come to know something. Students' individuality is used as a basis for appropriate teaching, rather than to rank and categorize learners. This vision of differences in learners demands more thorough information about those differences than a test score provides. What is needed are samples of student work that allow teachers to see what a child knows and is able to do, and how that knowledge and ability is applied to school learning. This need in classrooms has led to demand for use of performance tasks, projects, investigations, and portfolios as assessment tools.

The National Council of Teachers of Mathematics did not develop its standards for curriculum, for teaching, and for assessment in a vacuum (1989, 1993, 1995). These standards were developed in response to the cry that education was in need of tremendous reform. This cry was made by reports written by a number of groups, such as the National Commission on Excellence in Education (1983). Change is always difficult, but those who examine the entire story of the movement for reform in education will see that the changes that are being made will, ultimately, significantly enhance the quality of education available to America's children.

An optimist would say that a kind of synergy exists right now. As professionals have come to rethink curriculum and redefine what is important for students to learn, they have also reevaluated and modified their beliefs about how students learn. It is clear that the kind of assessment that is emerging in the field will complete the picture of needed reform. The portfolio—a purposeful collection that tells the story of a student's efforts, progress, or achievement in school—surely has an important place in that picture.

References

ANN ARBOR PUBLIC SCHOOLS (AAPS). 1993. *Alternative Assessment: Evaluating Student Performance in Elementary Mathematics.* Palo Alto, CA: Dale Seymour Publications.

BAKER, E. L., R. L. LINN, and J. L. HERMAN. 1996. "CRESST: A Continuing Mission to Improve Educational Assessment. *Evaluation Comment.*"Newsletter of UCLA's Center for the Study of Evaluation and The National Center for Research on Evaluation, Standards, and Student Testing.

BARON, M. A., and F. BOSCHEE. 1996. "Dispelling the Myths Surrounding OBE." *Phi Delta Kappan.* April: 574–576.

CHARLES, R., F. LESTER, and P. O'DAFFER. 1987. *How to Evaluate Progress in Problem Solving.* Reston, VA: National Council of Teachers of Mathematics.

CHITTENDEN, E. 1991. "Authentic Assessment, Evaluation, and Documentation of Student Performance." In *Expanding Student Assessment,* ed. V. Perrone. Alexandria, VA: Association for Supervision and Curriculum Development.

DEVRIES, R., AND L. KOHLBERG. 1987. *Constructivist Early Education: Overview and Comparisons with Other Programs.* Washington, DC: National Association for Education of Young Children.

ELBOW, P. 1994. "Will the Virtues of Portfolios Blind Us to Their Dangers?" In *New Directions in Portfolio Assessment,* ed. L. Black and D. Daiker. Portsmouth, NH: Boynton/Cook.

FIVE, C. L., and M. DIONISIO. 1996. *Bridging the Gap: Integrating*

Curriculum in Upper Elementary and Middle School. Portsmouth, NH: Heinemann.

GARCIA, E. G., and P. D. PEARSON. 1994. "Assessment and Diversity." *Review of Research in Education* 20: 337–392. Washington, DC: American Educational Research Association.

GLASER, R., and E. SILVER. 1994. "Assessment, Testing, and Instruction: Retrospect and Prospect." *Review of Research in Education.* 20: 393–422. Washington, DC: American Educational Research Association.

GLAZER, S. M., and S. B. BROWN. 1993. *Portfolios and Beyond: Collaborative Assessment in Reading and Writing.* Norwood, MA: Christopher-Gordon.

GRAVES, D. H., and B. S. SUNSTEIN, eds. 1992. *Portfolio Portraits.* Portsmouth, NH: Heinemann.

HARRIS FREEDMAN, R. L. 1994. *Open-Ended Questioning: A Handbook for Teachers.* Menlo Park, CA: Addison Wesley.

HYMES, D. L., A. E. CHAFIN, and P. GONDER. 1991. *The Changing Face of Testing and Assessment: Problems and Solutions.* Arlington, VA: American Association of School Administrators.

KATZ, L. G., and CHARD, S. C. 1994. *Engaging Children's Minds: The Project Approach.* Norwood, NJ: Ablex.

KLEIN, S. P., D. McCAFFREY, B. STECHER, and D. JORETZ. 1995. "The Reliability of Mathematics Portfolio Scores: Lessons from the Vermont Experience." *Applied Measurement* 8(3): 243–260.

KUHS, T. M. 1994. "Portfolio Assessment: Making It Work for the First Time." *Mathematics Teacher* 87(May): 332–335.

MANNING, M., G. MANNING, and R. LONG, 1994. *Theme Immersion: Inquiry-Based Curriculum in Elementary and Middle School.* Portsmouth, NH: Heinemann.

MARTIN, S. 1994. *Take a Look: Observation and Portfolio Assessment in Early Childhood.* Ontario: Addison Wesley.

MATHEMATICAL SCIENCE EDUCATION BOARD (MSEB). 1993. *Measuring Up: Prototypes for Mathematics Assessment.* Washington, DC: National Academy Press.

MEISELS, S. J. et al. 1994. *The Work Sampling System: An Overview.* Ann Arbor, MI: Rebus Planning Associates.

NATIONAL COMMISSION ON EXCELLENCE IN EDUCATION. 1983. *A Nation at Risk: The Imperative for Educational Reform.* Washington, DC: U.S. Government Printing Office.

NATIONAL COMMISSION ON TESTING AND PUBLIC POLICY (NCTPP). 1990. *From Gatekeeper to Gateway: Transforming Testing in America.* Chestnut Hill, MA: National Commission on Testing and Public Policy, Boston College.

NATIONAL COUNCIL OF TEACHERS OF MATHEMATICS (NCTM). 1989. *Curriculum and Evaluation Standards for School Mathematics.* Reston, VA: National Council of Teachers of Mathematics.

————. 1991. *Professional Standards for Teaching Mathematics.* Reston, VA: National Council of Teachers of Mathematics.

————. 1995. *Assessment Standards for School Mathematics.* Reston, VA: National Council of Teachers of Mathematics.

NATIONAL EDUCATION GOALS PANEL. 1996. *Profile of 1994–1995 State Assessment Systems and Reported Results.* Washington, DC: National Education Goals Panel.

NEILL, M. et al. 1995. *Implementing Performance Assessments: A Guide to Classroom, School, and System Reform.* Cambridge, MA: The National Center for Fair and Open Testing.

SHANNON, A., and J. S. ZAWOJEWKI. 1995. "Mathematics Performance Assessment: A New Game for Students." *The Mathematics Teacher* 88(9): 752–757.

SHORT, K. G. et al. 1996. *Learning Together Through Inquiry: From Columbus to Integrated Curriculum.* York, ME: Stenhouse.

SPANDEL, V., and R. CULHAM. 1994. *Creating a Portfolio: A Workshop Handout.* Portland, OR: Northwest Regional Education Laboratory.

STENMARK, J. K. 1989. *Assessment Alternatives in Mathematics.* Berkeley, CA: EQUALS, Lawrence Hall of Science, University of California.

STENMARK, J. K., ed. 1991. *Mathematics Assessment: Myths, Models, Good Questions, and Practical Suggestions.* Reston, VA: National Council of Teachers of Mathematics.

SWANSON, D. B., G. R. NORMAN, and R. L. LINN. 1995. Performance-

Based Assessment: Lessons from the Health Professions. *Educational Researcher* 24(5): 5–11.

TCHUDI, S., and S. LAFER. 1996. *The Interdisciplinary Teacher's Handbook: Integrated Teaching Across the Curriculum*. Portsmouth, NH: Boynton/Cook.

VANCE, J. H. 1982. "An Opinion Poll: A Percent Activity for All Students." In *Mathematics for the Middle Grades (5–9)*, ed. L. Silver and J. B. Smart. Reston, VA: National Council of Teachers of Mathematics.

VERMONT DEPARTMENT OF EDUCATION. 1991. *Looking Beyond "The Answer." Report of Vermont's Mathematics Portfolio Assessment Program*. Montpelier, VT: Vermont Department of Education.

WHITIN, D. J., H. MILLS, and T. O'KEEFE. 1990. *Living and Learning Mathematics: Stories and Strategies to Support Mathematics Literacy*. Portsmouth, NH: Heinemann.

WIGGINS, G. 1993. "Assessment: Authenticity, Context, and Validity." *Phi Delta Kappan*. November: 200–214.

WOLF, D., J. BIXBY, J. GLENN III, and H. GARDNER. 1991. "To Use Their Minds Well: Investigating New Forms of Student Assessment." *Review of Research in Education* 17. Washington, DC: American Educational Research Association.